Cambridge Elements

THE DYNAMIC METACAPABILITIES FRAMEWORK: INTRODUCING QUANTUM MANAGEMENT AND THE INFORMATIONAL VIEW OF THE FIRM

Harold Paredes-Frigolett
Diego Portales University

Andreas Pyka
University of Hohenheim

Shaftesbury Road, Cambridge CB2 8EA, United Kingdom

One Liberty Plaza, 20th Floor, New York, NY 10006, USA

477 Williamstown Road, Port Melbourne, VIC 3207, Australia

314–321, 3rd Floor, Plot 3, Splendor Forum, Jasola District Centre, New Delhi – 110025, India

103 Penang Road, #05–06/07, Visioncrest Commercial, Singapore 238467

Cambridge University Press is part of Cambridge University Press & Assessment, a department of the University of Cambridge.

We share the University's mission to contribute to society through the pursuit of education, learning and research at the highest international levels of excellence.

www.cambridge.org
Information on this title: www.cambridge.org/9781009627610

DOI: 10.1017/9781009627603

When citing this work, please include a reference to the DOI 10.1017/9781009627603

First published 2025

A catalogue record for this publication is available from the British Library

ISBN 978-1-009-62761-0 Hardback
ISBN 978-1-009-62763-4 Paperback
ISSN 2514-3573 (online)
ISSN 2514-3581 (print)

The Dynamic Metacapabilities Framework: Introducing Quantum Management and the Informational View of the Firm

Elements in Evolutionary Economics

DOI: 10.1017/9781009627603
First published online: January 2025

Harold Paredes-Frigolett
Diego Portales University

Andreas Pyka
University of Hohenheim

Author for correspondence: Harold Paredes-Frigolett, harold.paredes@udp.cl

Abstract: The view of dynamic capabilities in evolutionary economics as being based on capabilities comprised of routines has so far precluded their integration in evolutionary economics. This Element contributes to such integration by introducing the dynamic metacapabilities framework. Borrowing from quantum mechanics, dynamic metacapabilities assume that resources and capabilities, rather than being created ex-*nihilo*, result from bundles of information "decohering" to bundles of resources and capabilities as new information becomes available to the firm. Operationalized by a management paradigm we call "quantum management," dynamic metacapabilities contribute to integrating dynamic capabilities in evolutionary economics and to resolving the ongoing debate on what dynamic capabilities are by postulating an informational view of the firm according to which firms "evolve" with strategy throughout a lifecycle governing the transition from dynamic "metacapabilities" to dynamic capabilities and onto ordinary capabilities.

Keywords: Quantum management, ordinary capabilities, dynamic capabilities, dynamic metacapabilities, lifecycle of dynamic metacapabilties

JEL Classifications: O30, O31, O32, O33, O36

ISBNs: 9781009627610 (HB), 9781009627634 (PB), 9781009627603 (OC)
ISSNs: 2514-3573 (online), 2514-3581 (print)

Contents

1 Introduction

In this contribution, we introduce the dynamic metacapabilities framework as an initial step toward the ultimate goal of developing an informational theory of the firm. This framework extends dynamic capabilities, as proposed in the strategic management literature (Eisenhardt & Martin, 2000; Teece, Pisano, & Shuen, 1997), through higher-order dynamic capabilities. Referred to as dynamic metacapabilities, these higher-order dynamic capabilities endow firms with the flexibility required to deal with market, technological, and industry disruption, allowing them to drive and execute strategy under radical uncertainty (Kay & King, 2020) using a form of entrepreneurial management that is usually more difficult for incumbent firms to adopt. Borrowing from quantum mechanics and following a real options approach, we introduce a new management paradigm that we call "quantum management" to operationalize the dynamic metacapabilities framework proposed and to implement the type of entrepreneurial management advocated by the Teecean framework of dynamic capabilities (Teece, 2016).

1.1 Dynamic Capabilities and Entrepreneurial Management

Although the lack of flexibility of incumbents facing technological, market, or industry disruption is always an impediment for the adoption of the type of entrepreneurial management advocated by the Teecean dynamic capabilities framework (Teece, 2007), the problem of radically transforming a still successful business model arises for incumbents much earlier. Consider, for example, the sensing, seizing, and transforming dynamic capabilities proposed by the Teecean framework. While the sensing capabilities proposed by this framework are generally more readily available, the seizing and transforming capabilities proposed are more rare and difficult to implement. This is especially the case for incumbents, which often fail to execute radical business model transformations due to the dilemma of creative destruction such transformations entail (Christensen, 1997).

The lack of flexibility in the face of radical uncertainty is one of the main problems precluding incumbents from successfully deploying the seizing and transforming capabilities needed to deal with this dilemma (Kay & King, 2020; Teece, 2007). Unlike new business ventures that are more open to exploring, discovering, and implementing radical business model transformations, incumbents face complex trade-offs and usually opt for strategies with much lower levels of strategic uncertainty and organizational misalignment. However, seizing and transforming capabilities in highly dynamic markets often require that incumbents drive radical transformations in spite of the deep strategic uncertainty and organizational misalignment and the high opportunity costs these transformations entail (Kay & King, 2020). Such decisions are often delayed due to the high opportunity costs associated with transforming business models that still deliver value not only to the incumbents but also to key stakeholders in their innovation ecosystems, many of which are strategic allies in complex value chains that took these incumbents decades to form (Teece, 2007). This procrastinating behavior is observed even in cases of incumbents that successfully deployed the sensing capabilities needed to uncover the impending threats of technological, market, and industry disruption, which are characteristic of the entrepreneurial management proposed in connection with the dynamic capabilities framework in the strategic management literature (Helfat et al., 2007; Teece, 2016; Teece & Pisano, 1994; Teece, Pisano, & Shuen, 1990; Teece, Pisano, & Shuen 1997).

1.2 Overcoming the Pitfalls of Radical Business Model Transformations

In environments characterized by the type of radical uncertainty described by Kay & King (2020), incumbents often show a great deal of aversion to deploying seizing and transforming capabilities that radically change or even destroy their current business models. Incumbents often end up redoubling their efforts to perfect their current business models through incremental business model innovations instead of substantially or radically transforming them (Johnson, Christensen, & Kagermann, 2008). Such behavior often constitutes a strategic folly on the part of incumbents that results not in the intended preservation of their current business models but rather in delaying their demise while they still operate in the domain of gains. In such cases, the deployment of seizing and transforming capabilities comes often too late, as exemplified by Kodak and many other incumbents that failed to transform their business models in the face of technological, market, and industry disruption (Christensen, 1997).

While the high opportunity costs and the lack of flexibility contribute to explaining why incumbents fail to deploy the seizing and transforming capabilities needed to transform their business models under radical strategic uncertainty (Kay & King, 2020), empirical evidence suggests that incumbents also show anticannibalization proclivities that preclude them from transforming their business models while they still deliver gains. These anticannibalization proclivities of incumbents have been described by strategic management scholars and are connected with the dilemma of creative destruction (Teece, 2007). We conjecture that such a bias is governed by loss aversion as one of the main psychological effects rooted in the psychophysics of human decision-making under risk (Camerer, 2003, 2005; Frydman & Camerer, 2016). Indeed, the behavior shown by incumbents facing the dilemma of having to radically transform a still profitable business model is consistent with prospect theory, which would predict that the decisions of incumbents in environments ridden with deep strategic uncertainty are driven by a great deal of risk aversion while their business models still operate in the domain of gains (Kahneman & Tversky, 1979). According to this theory, incumbents would show the higher propensity to risk needed to radically transform their business models only after they have entered the domain of losses. From an evolutionary economics perspective, this change in decision-making behavior comes often too late (Christensen, 1997; Johnson, Christensen, & Kagermann, 2008).

The lack of strategies and decision-aiding tools allowing managers to deal with this bias against transforming a still successful business model is often the reason why incumbents resist radical business model transformations while their business models still operate in the domain of gains (Helfat et al., 2007; Teece, 2010, 2016). Given their potential to help managers make the complex decisions that are needed to seize and transform a successful business model under deep strategic uncertainty (Kay & King, 2020), the development of strategies, methodologies, and decision-aiding tools allowing incumbents to deal with this bias and avoid anticannibalization proclivities should be one of the main objectives of any dynamic capabilities framework (Teece, 2007, p. 1334). Such an undertaking would contribute not only to operationalizing dynamic capabilities frameworks (Eisenhardt & Martin, 2000; Teece, 2007) but also to developing general theory of the entrepreneurial firm (Teece, 2016).

1.3 Competitive Advantage and the Value of Cooperation

While the deployment of decision-aiding methodologies inspired in the psychology of decision-making under risk (Kahneman & Tversky, 1979; Tversky & Kahneman, 1992) is needed to avoid the pitfalls associated with radical business model transformations on the part of incumbents, the deployment of "coopeting" strategies is essential for the operationalization of the type of capabilities needed to deal with radical business model transformations. Such strategies are particularly important when dealing with radical business model transformations in knowledge-intensive industries dominated by rapid market, industry, and technological change. In such industries, competing firms often deploy coopeting strategies to reduce the potential negative outcomes of investment decisions made under radical uncertainty and these coopeting strategies often follow oblique, as opposed to direct, innovation pathways (Kay & King, 2020).

If we assume that the competitive advantage is the essence of any business model and that any competitive advantage is predicated upon a unique and compelling value proposition, it follows that the way value is transferred, that is, delivered, in a complex value chain will characterize the different business models of the participants in that value chain (Teece, 1976, 2010). While firms embedded in knowledge-intensive industries tend to adopt competitive strategies in complex industry value chains during periods of continuity and low strategic uncertainty, in periods of high discontinuity there seems to be the need to embrace a different array of coopeting strategies to deploy seizing and transforming capabilities under deep uncertainty (Foster, 1986b). During such periods of high disruption, the ability to redefine entire value chains by transferring value among otherwise competing firms gains unprecedented importance (Pisano, Shan, & Teece, 1988).[1]

The venture capital industry provides one of the most relevant cases of deploying such coopeting strategies. In that industry, deals are syndicated among otherwise competing venture capital firms to deal with deep strategic uncertainty. In order to be effective, deal syndication requires that a critical mass of competing venture capital firms be available in complex innovation networks (Ahrweiler, 2010). As a coopeting strategy, deal syndication is of the essence to sustain the otherwise unviable business model of the venture capital industry (Sorenson & Stuart, 2001, 2008). The radical business model innovations driven by venture capitalists tend to create situations that prompt them to deploy coopeting strategies in order to gain the flexibility required to deal with deep strategic uncertainty (Pisano, Shan, & Teece, 1988). The case of the venture capital industry highlights the need to add coopeting strategies as a key microfoundation of the dynamic capabilities framework (Teece, 2007).

1.4 Quantum Management and Dynamic Metacapabilities

In this contribution, we set out the dynamic metacapabilities framework and operationalize it using a novel management paradigm that we call "quantum management." Inspired by quantum mechanics and based on a lifecycle of "dynamic metacapabilities," quantum management is operationalized through three classes of real options that mimic quantum-mechanical effects to deal with radical uncertainty and organizational misalignment (Kay & King, 2020).

[1] An example of this is the cooperation model adopted in the pharmaceutical industry, which was the result of the emergence of molecular biology as the new technological paradigm in this industry during the late 1990s and early 2000s (Pyka & Saviotti, 2005).

Operationalized by this new quantum management paradigm, the dynamic metacapabilities framework proposed departs from the standard resource-based view of the firm by dropping its implicit assumption that resources and capabilities are created ex nihilo (Barney, 1991; Penrose, 1995; Wernerfelt, 1984) and enables an informational, as opposed to a resource-based, view of the firm (Wernerfelt, 1984).

Following such an innovation lifecycle approach, quantum management allows firms to deploy strategies to cope with varying degrees of strategic uncertainty and organizational misalignment as their business models transition throughout the lifecycle of dynamic metacapabilities. As the strategic uncertainty and organizational misalignment in the internal and external environment of the firm decrease, dynamic metacapabilities "decohere"[2] to lower-order dynamic capabilities (Eisenhardt & Martin, 2000; Teece, 2007) and eventually to ordinary capabilities (Barney, 1991; Mahoney & Pandian, 1992). Such a lifecycle approach allows the dynamic metacapabilities framework to integrate the higher-order dynamic metacapabilities needed by firms to drive strategy under radical strategic uncertainty and organizational misalignment (Kay & King, 2020) with the lower-order dynamic capabilities (Eisenhardt & Martin, 2000; Teece, 2007) and the ordinary capabilities (Barney, 1991; Penrose, 1995; Wernerfelt, 1984) needed by firms to operate in high-velocity and moderately dynamic markets, respectively.

1.5 Toward an Informational Theory of the Firm

An important goal of the dynamic metacapabilities framework proposed, and the new quantum management paradigm used to implement it, is to propose an informational theory of the firm. Quantum management operationalizes dynamic metacapabilities following a real options approach that mimics quantum-mechanical effects to deal with radical uncertainty and organizational misalignment. Quantum management implements the kind of entrepreneurial management envisioned by the Teecean dynamic capabilities framework (Teece, 2007) and represents not only a theoretical contribution. Quantum management also represents a practical contribution in that it can endow entrepreneurial managers with dynamic metacapabilities that mimic quantum-mechanical effects in order to deal with radical strategic uncertainty and

[2] According to the Copenhagen interpretation of quantum mechanics, decoherence refers to the process that results from the interaction of a quantum-mechanical system with a classical system, for example when a measurement (observation) is made, which causes the system not only to become entangled with its environment but also to lose some of its quantum-mechanical properties.

organizational misalignment (Kay & King, 2020), allowing them to execute corporate and business strategies during periods of high market, technological, and industry disruption.

1.6 Dynamic Capabilities and Evolutionary Economics

As noted by Teece (2023), evolutionary models of the firm generally assume that dynamic capabilities are merely routines (Nelson & Winter, 1982, p. 17). These models focus on continuity (Nelson, 1991; Winter, 2003, 2006) and highlight the bounded rationality of managers (Nelson & Winter, 1982, p. 32), as opposed to focusing on their entrepreneurial management skills (Teece, 2018c). More importantly, evolutionary models of the firm regard technology as the driver of primarily incremental innovations aimed not at shaping the environment but rather at responding to it (Nelson, 2018, p. 24).

Dynamic capabilities, as conceptualized by Teece (2007) almost two decades after this framework was originally introduced (Teece, Pisano, & Shuen, 1990), depart from the general view of evolutionary economists who construe firm evolution as a process of implementing incremental changes based on dynamic capabilities to adapt to a changing environment. According to this view, dynamic capabilities comprise new routines, or combinations of existing routines, that are eminently “local.” As opposed to this generally accepted view of dynamic capabilities among evolutionists, the characterization of dynamic capabilities proposed by the Teecean framework highlights their “non-locality” and their focus on a more radical, intentional, and directed form of evolution not aimed at responding to changes in the environment but rather at shaping it.[3]

Rather than assuming that technology is the main driver of innovation, the Teecean framework of dynamic capabilities considers that entrepreneurial management takes center stage as a catalyst of radical innovations aimed at shaping the environment. According to this framework, dynamic capabilities along three distinct categories, namely, “sensing,” “seizing,” and “transforming,” enable a type of entrepreneurial management predicated on a multidimensional construct comprising not just the technological but also the market and business models dimensions, to which the temporal dimension should also be added (Teece, 2023, p. 210). The Teecean framework thus assumes that dynamic capabilities, as opposed to ordinary capabilities, comprise entrepreneurial and leadership skills that are deployed following a top-down approach. Such top-down approach “lies outside the purview of evolutionary

[3] Teece refers to it as “evolution with design, purpose, and strategy” (Teece, 2023, p. 215).

economics" (Teece, 2023, p. 215), which assumes that dynamic capabilities are rather deployed in a bottom-up and undirected manner.[4]

1.7 Filling the Gap

There is today no consensus about what dynamic capabilities are among strategic management scholars, on the one hand, and evolutionary economists, on the other. This lack of consensus becomes evident in the concluding remarks of David Teece's recent essay about dynamic capabilities and evolutionary economics (Teece, 2023, p. 215), in which he states: "I hope by viewing evolutionary economics within the broader context of the dynamic capabilities framework, evolutionary economists will be better able to handle a fuller range of innovations and non-routine entrepreneurial decisions."

As noted by strategic management scholars endorsing competing views on what dynamic capabilities are (Eisenhardt & Martin, 2000), the level of underspecification and lack of operationalization of the Teecean dynamic capabilities framework has so far rendered it rather "tautological and vague" (Eisenhardt & Martin, 2000, p. 1106). This lack of operationalization is also a major impediment to fulfilling Teece's hope of bringing the full potential of dynamic capabilities to fruition in the field of evolutionary economics.

Our aim is to contribute to filling this gap by introducing the dynamic metacapabilities framework. Operationalized through "quantum management" as a new management paradigm inspired by quantum mechanics, dynamic metacapabilities shall contribute to reconciling not only the diverging views on what dynamic capabilities are held today by evolutionary economists and strategic management scholars but also the two most influential and competing views on dynamic capabilities among strategic management scholars.

1.8 Organization of Our Contribution

Our contribution starts with a review of the relevant literature in business model innovation and dynamic capabilities our dynamic metacapabilities framework draws upon. Our review includes diverging views on what dynamic capabilities are held by evolutionary economists and strategic management scholars.

We then introduce the dynamic metacapabilities framework. Inspired by quantum mechanics, we describe the lifecycle of dynamic metacapabilities governing the transition from dynamic metacapabilities to dynamic and ultimately to ordinary capabilities. We analyze the difference between ordinary and dynamic capabilities, the difference between the two main competing views

[4] A sort of "evolution without design, purpose, and strategy."

on dynamic capabilities in the strategic management research community, and the difference between the dynamic capabilities and dynamic metacapabilities frameworks. We also explain how the dynamic metacapabilities framework, and its operationalization through quantum management, contributes to reconciling the competing views on what dynamic capabilities are in the evolutionary economics and strategic management research communities.

We then introduce quantum management, a novel management paradigm that operationalizes the dynamic metacapabilities framework following a real options approach. Based on three classes of real options that mimic quantum-mechanical effects such as superpositioning, entanglement, and tunneling, quantum management allows firms to deal with the type of radical strategic uncertainty and organizational misalignment that is pervasive in rapidly changing environments. Quantum management mimics processes of quantum decoherence and proposes that dynamic metacapabilities decohere to actual dynamic capabilities, and ultimately to ordinary capabilities, as new information reducing the radical uncertainty and organizational misalignment in the environment of the firm becomes available (Kay & King, 2020).

Next, we discuss the main contributions of the dynamic metacapabilities framework and its operationalization through quantum management and describe how they lead to an informational, as opposed to a resource-based, view of the firm. We show how dynamic and ordinary capabilities are not created ex nihilo but are rather the result of dynamic metacapabilities decohering from the pure informational realm of metacapabilities, construed as potential bundles of information aimed at achieving evolutionary fitness, to the realm of actual dynamic capabilities and ultimately ordinary capabilities aimed at achieving technical fitness. We also present a real-life example that describes quantum management and dynamic metacapabilities at work in environments ridden with radical uncertainty and organizational misalignment.

We conclude that the informational view of the firm underlying the dynamic metacapabilities framework not only constitutes a departure from mainstream approaches in strategic management and evolutionary economics rooted in the resource-based view of the firm but is also better equipped to capture the dynamics of the kind of business model transformations that are of the essence for firms seeking evolutionary fitness in rapidly changing environments subject to radical strategic uncertainty and organizational misalignment.

2 Previous Work

We now present a review of the literature on business models, business model innovation, and dynamic capabilities our dynamic metacapabilities framework draws upon.

2.1 Business Models

In their review of extant literature on business models, Massa, Tucci, and Afuah (2017, pp. 77–78) identified a first category of contributions whose focus is on the components of business models and how they map different attributes of firms, including the revenue model (Birkinshaw & Goddard, 2009; Gambardella & McGahan, 2010), the value proposition and the process of value capture (Bocken, Rana, & Short, 2015; Roome & Louche, 2016), the delivery model (San Román et al., 2011, Sinfield et al., 2012; Weill, Malone, & Apel, 2011), the competitive strategy (Casadesus-Masanell & Zhu, 2013), the firm strategy (Dahan et al., 2010; Hienerth, Keinz, & Lettl, 2011; Smith, Binns, & Tushman, 2010), and other components of the business model (Chesbrough, 2010; Nielsen & Lund, 2014). Yet few contributions focus on designing business models (Zott & Amit, 2010) or on how incumbents can adopt new business models (Markides & Oyon, 2010).

Another stream of research in the business model literature focuses on the study of business models as cognitive structures and involve scholarly work that construes business models not as real objects but as models (Aspara et al., 2013; Baden-Fuller & Morgan, 2010), including models conveying the logic of the firm (Chesbrough & Rosensbloom, 2002; Doganova & Eyquem-Renault, 2009) and models of the interface of the firm with its environment (Doz & Kosonen, 2010), or as narratives (Magretta, 2002), or as mental models (Martins, Rindova, & Greenbaum, 2015), or as aids for decision-making (Velu & Stiles, 2013).

A third stream of literature focuses on the study formal representations of business models. This third stream is relevant because it lends itself to an operationalization of business models and to the definition of methodologies and tools for managerial decision-making. This stream of research includes work on formal representations of some of the components of business models such as the revenue model (Abdelkafi & Täuscher, 2016; Itami & Nishino, 2010), the logic of the firm (Casadesus-Masanell & Ricart, 2010; Upward & Jones, 2015), the value proposition and the process of creation, delivery, and capture of value (Demil & Lecocq, 2010; Reim, Parida, & Örtqvist, 2015; Yunus, Moingeon, & Lehmann-Ortega, 2010; Wirtz, Schilke, & Ullrich, 2010; Schaltegger, Hansen, & Lüdecke-Freund 2016), the competitive advantage (McGrath, 2010), the ecosystem of the firm (Wells, 2016), as well as formal representations of other components of business models (Baden-Fuller & Haefliger, 2013; Boons & Lüdecke-Freund 2013; Osterwalder, Pigneur, & Tucci, 2005; Provance, Donnely, & Carayannis, 2011).

None of these three approaches to business model research has addressed the dynamics of business model creation. Whether this scholarly research is based on the attributes, cognitive structures, or formal representations approaches to business models, its aim has been to describe business models as static objects. This body of scholarly research has not yet described the different phases and stages in the process that leads to their creation. Although some of the scholarly work cited previously has addressed the interface between strategy and business models (Casadesus-Masanell & Ricart, 2010), the integration of modern strategic management frameworks such as dynamic capabilities with business model formation has been discussed by few authors rather sketchily (Teece, 2010). By and large, the needed operationalization of dynamic capabilities and their integration with business model research is still missing in the strategic management literature.

2.2 Business Model Innovation

Radical business model innovation involves singular events causing firms to develop the kind of capabilities proposed by the dynamic capabilities framework (Teece, 2007). Empirical evidence suggests that leading firms that are generally good at sensing opportunities and threats also generally fail to seize opportunities or neutralize threats when they involve introducing radical innovations to a hitherto successful business model (Christensen, 1997). The failure to do so is due to the inability of incumbents to transform complementary and cospecialized tangible and intangible assets that took them decades to build, configure, and reconfigure in open innovation systems (Teece, 2007).

From the perspective of conventional strategic management frameworks rooted not only in the resource-based view of the firm (Barney, 1991; Penrose, 1995; Wernerfelt, 1984) but also in the positioning framework (Porter, 2008), such incumbents cannot be regarded as firms that failed to execute the strategies indicated by these frameworks, which would have indeed consisted of strategies aiming to protect VRIN[5] resources and capabilities, instead of radically transforming them. Work on vertical integration (Macher & Mowery, 2005; Pisano, Shan, & Teece, 1988; Teece, 1976; Winter, 2003) and business models, business strategy, and innovation (Teece, 2010) seem to corroborate how difficult it is to deal with the dilemma of having to transform complementary and cospecialized tangible and intangible assets tightly integrated in complex industry value chains to neutralize a threat or seize an opportunity. The analysis of cases of radical business model innovation reveals that incumbents, unlike new business ventures (Foster, 1986a), often fail to adopt the kind of entrepreneurial management needed to avoid falling into this trap (Christensen, 1997; Teece, 2016).

[5] VRIN is an acronym that stands for valuable, rare, inimitable and non-substitutable.

The innovation economics and management literature provides us with plenty of cases of incumbent firms that were unable to seize opportunities and manage threats when facing major market disruption due to their failure to redefine their business models (Christensen, 1997; Pisano, Shan, & Teece, 1988; Teece, 1976; Winter, 2003). From a dynamic capabilities framework perspective, the failure to do so is ultimately due to the inability of incumbents to reconfigure the components of a hitherto successful business model (Amit & Zott, 2001; Johnson, Christensen, & Kagermann, 2008; Osterwalder & Pigneur, 2010; Ritter, 2014). These cases are all related to the dilemma of creative destruction (Schumpeter, 1942) and confirm that global market leaders often fail to keep their dominance when challenged by the disruptive technology of smaller competitors (Foster, 1986a).

Also noteworthy are cases of incumbents that were unable to deal with the dilemma of creative destruction due not to a threat posed by technological or market disruption (Foster, 1986b) but rather to their unwillingness to cooperate with a strategic partner that presented an opportunity for radical innovation requiring that they reconfigure their hitherto successful business model. Such cases bring to our attention an important dynamic capability, namely, the ability to cooperate with firms that are regarded as competitors during periods of industry disruption (Paredes-Frigolett & Pyka, 2015).

The ability to cooperate during periods of industry disruption is an important microfoundation of the dynamic capabilities framework (Teece, 2007) that has so far been rather neglected despite the comprehensive body of scholarly work on cooperation via strategic alliances in the business model literature (Amit & Zott, 2001; Johnson, Christensen, & Kagermann, 2008; Osterwalder & Pigneur, 2010; Ritter, 2014). Although the role of cooperation in the process of value creation is widely recognized today (Casadesus-Masanell & Ricart, 2010; Chesbrough & Rosensbloom, 2002; Pyka, 2002), scholars have paid less attention to the role that cooperation plays during processes of radical business model innovation as a vehicle allowing managers to deal with the transformation of a still successful and profitable business model (Chesbrough, 2007; Markides & Sosa, 2013; Teece, 2016) in environments subject to radical uncertainty (Kay & King, 2020).

2.3 Two Competing Dynamic Capabilities Frameworks

The reconceptualization of dynamic capabilities proposed by Eisenhardt and Martin (2000, p. 1111) constitutes quite a departure from the traditional view of dynamic capabilities, as originally proposed by Teece, Pisano, & Shuen (1997) and explicated in more detail by Teece (2007). In particular, the reconceptualization of dynamic capabilities proposed by Eisenhardt and Martin (2000, p. 1111) differs from the traditional view in that dynamic capabilities:

1. are defined by "specific organizational and strategic processes" instead of "routines to learn routines";
2. present "commonalities with some idiosyncratic details across firms" instead of being "idiosyncratic and firm specific";
3. are "detailed and analytic routines in moderately dynamic markets" but "simple and experiential in high-velocity markets";
4. are "predictable in moderately dynamic markets" but "unpredictable in high-velocity markets";
5. provide a source of competitive advantage but not of sustained competitive advantage because they are "somewhat rare, equifinal, substitutable, and fungible" instead of "rare, inimitable and non-substitutable"; and
6. evolve not following a "unique path" but rather a "unique path shaped by learning mechanisms."

An important difference between the reconceptualization of dynamic capabilities proposed by Eisenhardt and Martin (2000, p. 1113) and the traditional view of dynamic capabilities[6] is that dynamic capabilities can only obtain a "temporary competitive advantage" due to their "substitutability and fungibility and the imitable nature of best practices within an industry" (Eisenhardt & Martin, 2000, p. 1106). Another important difference is the claim made by Eisenhardt and Martin (2000, p. 1113) that the "traditional view of dynamic capabilities collapses in high-velocity markets."[7]

2.4 Business Model Transformation

The framework proposed by Teece, Pisano, & Shuen (1997) seems more attuned to being deployed in phases of a lifecycle aimed at implementing substantial and radical business model transformations under deep strategic uncertainty. The Teecean dynamic capabilities framework requires that firms deploy sensing, seizing, and transforming capabilities, which are the three main categories of dynamic capabilities proposed by Teece, Pisano, & Shuen (1997) that are assumed to be sources of "sustainable enterprise performance" in rapidly changing environments (Teece, 2007, p. 1319).[8] More than actual

[6] Which subsumes the framework of dynamic capabilities originally proposed by Teece, Pisano, & Shuen (1997) and is explicated in more detail by Teece (2007).

[7] This acknowledges the role market dynamism has in a dynamic capabilities framework.

[8] In the present context, sustainable enterprise performance can be considered to be equivalent to sustainable competitive advantage.

capabilities, however, sensing, seizing and transforming stand for general categories or families of capabilities. Although Teece (2007, p. 1342) propose some microfoundations under each of these categories, a comprehensive list of dynamic capabilities are not listed explicitly in the Teecean framework. The concept of lifecycle is not stated explicitly in this framework either, although there is an inherent lifecycle associated with the categories of sensing, seizing and transforming.

According to Eisenhardt and Martin (2000), dynamic capabilities are not new and strategic management scholars can benefit from reviewing the comprehensive body of research that exists today on a wide range of (dynamic) capabilities in concrete management areas such as new product development or strategic alliances. In describing what dynamic capabilities are, Eisenhardt and Martin (2000) follow an empirically grounded approach. This empirical approach differs from the conceptual approach followed by Teece (2007) in that Eisenhardt and Martin (2000) describe a number of concrete capabilities rather than postulating different classes of capabilities. While the Teecean approach to describing dynamic capabilities is thus primarily conceptual, the approach followed by Eisenhardt and Martin (2000) is primarily empirical. However, these authors do not come up with a taxonomy of dynamic capabilities following an empirical-to-conceptual approach or with a typology of dynamic capabilities following a conceptual-to-empirical approach (Nickerson, Varshney, & Muntermann, 2013).

Eisenhardt and Martin (2000) propose that dynamic capabilities are not path dependent but rather equifinal,[9] which is a result of the substitutability of dynamic capabilities. The fungibility of dynamic capabilities makes them also inadequate to serve as sources of sustainable competitive advantage, as any competitive advantage achieved through them would be short-lived and could only lead to a temporary competitive advantage (D'Aveni, 1994; D'Aveni, Dagnino, & Smith, 2010). This is quite a departure from the ordinary capabilities that are usually deployed in moderately dynamic markets, in which a sustainable competitive advantage can be achieved through VRIN capabilities, as proposed by mainstream strategic management frameworks rooted in the resourced-based view of the firm (Barney, 1991; Penrose, 1959; Wernerfelt, 1984, 1995).

While the dynamic capabilities postulated by Teece, Pisano, & Shuen (1997) focus on introducing and implementing strategy that can result in radical

[9] The principle of equifinality assumes that competing firms in an industry can end up achieving the same strategic objective following different pathways.

business model transformations under deep strategic uncertainty in the pursuit of evolutionary as opposed to technical fitness, the dynamic capabilities postulated by Eisenhardt and Martin (2000) do not address such radical business model transformations specifically and seem more attuned to implementing changes to an existing strategy by introducing incremental or substantial business model innovations, for example through the adoption of best practices. While in moderately dynamic markets the dynamic capabilities proposed by Eisenhardt and Martin (2000, p. 1115) focus on technical fitness, in high-velocity markets they commence to shift their focus to evolutionary fitness as the strategic uncertainty in the environment of the firm increases. This is reflected in the "ambiguous industry structure" in which they operate, which is characterized by "blurred business models, ambiguous and shifting players, and nonlinear and unpredictable change."

However, the original focus on technical fitness of the type of dynamic capabilities needed in moderately dynamic markets is not entirely relinquished in high-velocity markets, as evidenced by the claim that "dynamic capabilities in high-velocity markets can be construed as best practices across firms" (Eisenhardt & Martin, 2000, p. 1116). Although they retain this partial focus on the kind of technical fitness that is characteristic of the ordinary capabilities based on VRIN resources and capabilities (Wernerfelt, 1984), the dynamic capabilities Eisenhardt and Martin (2000, p. 1111) postulate for high-velocity markets do not correspond to ordinary but rather to dynamic capabilities that are either imitable[10] or substitutable,[11] and ultimately equifinal.

2.5 Dynamic Capabilities in Evolutionary Economics

The big disconnect between the two competing dynamic capabilities frameworks is in great part the result of strategic management scholars having failed to provide a formal framework able to incorporate the "dynamics" of business model transformation into a, *nomen est omen,* "dynamic" capabilities framework. We argue that the lack of such dynamics in the two competing dynamic capabilities frameworks has also precluded the integration of dynamic capabilities, with its view of seeking evolutionary fitness as evolution with design, purpose, and strategy (Teece, 2023), into evolutionary economics.

We propose that the ongoing debate on what dynamic capabilities are can be settled, and the integration of dynamic capabilities into evolutionary economics can be undertaken, by adopting a lifecycle approach that incorporates the dynamics of business model innovation and transformation into a more

[10] Such as the adoption of best industry practices.

[11] Which therefore renders them not entirely path dependent.

general dynamic metacapabilities framework. According to this view, whenever firms deploy dynamic capabilities to adopt the kind of entrepreneurial management that is characteristic of new business ventures, they need to undertake business model innovations and transformations that are governed by an innovation lifecycle comprising phases and stages exhibiting different degrees of deep strategic uncertainty and organizational misalignment (Kay & King, 2020).

Although previous scholarly work on dynamic capabilities had already introduced the concept of capability lifecycles in the context of the dynamic resource-based view of the firm (Helfat & Peteraf, 2003), a lifecycle approach to dynamic metacapabilities that delimits the objectives of each phase of the lifecycle, and the type of dynamic metacapabilities and dynamic and ordinary capabilities needed in each phase, is still missing. Filling this important gap is required not only to shed light on what dynamic capabilities are and to settle the still ongoing debate on the two competing approaches to dynamic capabilities in the strategic management literature (Eisenhardt & Martin, 2000; Teece, 2007) but also to fulfill the more ambitious goal of integrating the full potential of dynamic capabilities into evolutionary economics, as envisioned by Teece (2023). Key to achieving these goals is the integration of the "dynamics" of business model transformation into a dynamic metacapabilities framework and the realization that these two approaches to dynamic capabilities operate at different levels, pursue different objectives, and are deployed during different phases of a general lifecycle we refer to as the "the lifecycle of dynamic metacapabilities."

The type of ordinary and dynamic capabilities and dynamic metacapabilities deployed by entrepreneurial firms will depend on the phase of the lifecycle of dynamic metacapabilities they are in. In a phase ridden with radical uncertainty and organizational misalignment (Kay & King, 2020), firms will need to deploy dynamic metacapabilities endowing them with the greatest degree of flexibility required to navigate through "a sea of potentialities" in the pursuit of evolutionary fitness (Teece, 2007). Once firms enter a phase in which the strategic uncertainty and organizational misalignment have been reduced, they will need to deploy the kind of imitable, substitutable, and equifinal dynamic capabilities that have been proposed by Eisenhardt & Martin (2000) for high-velocity markets in the pursuit of both evolutionary and technical fitness.

Finally, if firms enter a phase characterized by moderate strategic uncertainty and organization misalignment, they will need to deploy the kind of "ordinary capabilities" proposed by mainstream strategic management frameworks for moderately dynamic markets in the pursuit of technical fitness (Barney, 1991; Penrose, 1959; Wernerfelt, 1984, 1995).

3 The Dynamic Metacapabilities Framework

While ordinary capabilities reign supreme in stable environments subject to moderate changes in the external and internal environment of the firm, they begin to collapse in environments that are more dynamic. This corresponds to the boundary condition proposed by Eisenhardt & Martin (2000, p. 1106) in high-velocity markets. In such environments, the deployment of dynamic capabilities is necessary to cope with higher levels of strategic uncertainty and organizational misalignment (Eisenhardt & Martin, 2000; Teece, 2007). Dynamic metacapabilities, on the other hand, are needed whenever the external and internal environment of the firm shows very high degrees of strategic uncertainty and organizational misalignment (Kay & King, 2020).

3.1 The Lifecycle of Dynamic Metacapabilities

The lifecycle dynamic metacapabilities governs the transition from ordinary capabilities to dynamic capabilities and onto dynamic metacapabilities and is shown in Figure 1.

3.1.1 The "Decoherence" of Dynamic Metacapabilities and Dynamic Capabilities

Dynamic metacapabilities are intended to implement very high degrees of flexibility. At this metalevel, firms can be construed as bundles of information that have the potential to manifest themselves as actual resources, capabilities and competencies. Whenever the strategic uncertainty and organizational misalignment in the external and internal environment of the firm are reduced

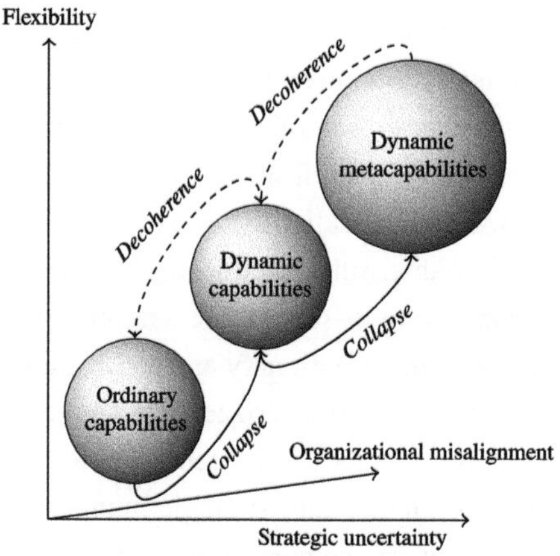

Figure 1 The lifecycle of dynamic metacapabilities

from very high to high levels and then from high levels to moderate and low levels, dynamic metacapabilities "decohere" to dynamic capabilities and dynamic capabilities decohere to ordinary capabilities, respectively. Such process of "decoherence" is shown using sloped thick dashed lines in Figure 1.

Inspired by the process of decoherence in quantum mechanics (Sakurai & Napolitano, 2020; Zeh, 1970) that occurs when a quantum-mechanical system of subatomic particles gets entangled with its environment and loses coherent superpositions (Vasallo & Romano, 2023),[12] the process of "decoherence" shown in Figure 1 represents a boundary condition that governs the transition from a state involving all strategic options available to the firm, construed as the superposition of all possible strategic options, to a subset of instantiated strategic options that are obtained after making a measurement.

In the dynamic metacapabilities framework, such measurements can be construed as processes of exploration that take place as business model innovations and transformations unfold throughout the lifecycle of dynamic metacapabilities shown in Figure 1. Such processes of exploration are intended for the environment, which in our case corresponds to the firm, to gain information about the system under observation, which in our case corresponds to the set of all strategic options that are only "potentially" available to the firm. From an information science (Shannon, 1948) and a quantum information science perspective (Zeh, 1970), while decoherence allows the environment to gain information about the system comprising the measured quantum correlations, it also leads the system to lose information to the environment, which has now access to a reduced set of decohered states that have been lost in the system by virtue of it having decohered as a result of its entanglement with the environment. So long as the system under observation has not yet decohered, the firm can benefit from deploying dynamic metacapabilities allowing it to entertain all potential strategic options in parallel. But as the processes of exploration transition into processes of discovery, the system begins to decohere, which has as a result that the firm has no longer access to the set of all potential strategic options. As a result of decoherence, however, the firm gains enough information about a subset of strategic options, which can now be instantiated and implemented through lower-order dynamic capabilities.

As opposed to dynamic metacapabilities, dynamic capabilities are not intended to implement very high degrees of flexibility and they do not operate in the purely informational realm of dynamic metacapabilities. As bundles of

[12] For example, through its interaction with a classical system set up to make a measurement of certain properties of the quantum-mechanical system.

information decohere to bundles of resources, capabilities, and competencies within the firm, dynamic metacapabilities decohere to dynamic capabilities. As this process unfolds, the focus of dynamic metacapabilities begins to gradually shift from the pursuit of evolutionary fitness, which is more characteristic of the transformative dynamic capabilities proposed by Teece (2007), to evolutionary and technical fitness, which is more characteristic of the dynamic capabilities proposed by Eisenhardt & Martin (2000). While the transition of dynamic metacapabilities into dynamic capabilities is governed by a process of decoherence that operates at a purely informational level and is aimed at converting bundles of information into emergent bundles of resources, capabilities, and competencies as a result of innovation processes of exploration and discovery, the transition of dynamic into ordinary capabilities is governed by a process of decoherence that operates at an informational level on emergent bundles of resources, capabilities, and competencies with the aim of further developing and ultimately leveraging them during the phase of exploitation.

As this process of decoherence unfolds throughout the lifecycle of dynamic metacapabilities, information is transformed into new knowledge. Defined as new valuable uses that are discovered for new information obtained through dynamic metacapabilities and dynamic capabilities,[13] new knowledge allows the firm to reduce the strategic uncertainty and organizational misalignment from high to medium levels, which leads to the emergence of best practices as a result of incremental innovations within entrepreneurial firms. The process of adoption of these best practices across firms within an industry leads to a type of dynamic capabilities with a blended focus on technical and evolutionary fitness and correspond to those postulated by Eisenhardt and Martin (2000).

Whenever the strategic uncertainty and organizational misalignment in the external and internal environment of the firm decrease from high and medium levels to moderate and low levels, dynamic capabilities decohere to ordinary capabilities. Ordinary capabilities manifest themselves as actual consolidated bundles of resources, capabilities, and competencies within the firm and focus on technical as opposed to evolutionary fitness (Barney, 1991; Penrose, 1959; Wernerfelt, 1984, 1995). In such environments, the strategic uncertainty and organizational misalignment have been significantly reduced so that corporate, business, and functional strategies can now be executed in such a way as to achieve not only strategic but also organizational alignment within the new organizational structure of the firm (Carlson & Wilmot, 2006). While the

[13] This definition is based on the more generic definition provided by Devlin (1999).

process of decoherence unfolds from dynamic metacapabilities to dynamic capabilities and ultimately to ordinary capabilities, the process of "collapse," shown in Figure 1 using sloped thick black lines, unfolds in the opposite direction.

3.1.2 The Collapse of Ordinary and Dynamic Capabilities

Ordinary capabilities become ineffective whenever the external environment of the firm transitions from low and moderate levels to high levels of strategic uncertainty and organizational misalignment. This boundary condition was introduced by Eisenhardt & Martin (2000, p. 1106) and states that the ordinary capabilities postulated by the resource-based view of the firm (Barney, 1991; Penrose, 1959; Wernerfelt, 1984, 1995) break down in high-velocity markets. To the extent that the changes to the existing strategy are moderate, a readjusted strategy may be executed within the existing organizational structure of the firm by introducing slight changes to the current business model through ordinary capabilities. However, if such changes occur in rapidly changing environments, then ordinary capabilities start to collapse, which makes it necessary for firms to deploy dynamic capabilities to drive strategy in "high-velocity" markets (Eisenhardt & Martin, 2000, p. 1106).

According to the resource-based view of the firm (Barney, 1991; Nelson, 1991; Penrose, 1959; Peteraf, 1993; Wernerfelt, 1984, 1995), when firms operate in moderately dynamic markets the pursuit of a sustainable competitive advantage can be predicated on ordinary capabilities comprising VRIN resources, capabilities, and competencies. In high-velocity markets, however, Eisenhardt & Martin (2000, p. 1106) postulate that the pursuit of a sustainable competitive advantage should be replaced with the pursuit of a temporary competitive advantage. This is consistent with the view endorsed by strategic management scholars studying highly dynamic markets in hypercompetitive industries, as described by D'Aveni (1994) and D'Aveni, Dagnino, & Smith (2010). This is quite a departure from the Teecean dynamic capabilities, which Teece (2007, p. 1319) defines as those allowing firms to "achieve sustainable performance."

As ordinary capabilities collapse due to increasing strategic uncertainty and organizational misalignment in the environment of the firm, processes of discovery through dynamic capabilities will need to be deployed. Likewise, as further increases in strategic uncertainty and organizational misalignment in the environment of the firm cause dynamic capabilities to collapse, processes of exploration through dynamic metacapabilities will need to be deployed. These processes of collapse unfold throughout the lifecycle of dynamic metacapabilities shown in Figure 1 as the strategic uncertainty and organizational misalignment transition from low and moderate levels to high and very high levels.

On the other hand, once dynamic metacapabilities have decohered to dynamic capabilities and dynamic capabilities have decohered to new bundles of ordinary capabilities with their focus on technical fitness, these new ordinary capabilities will drive exploitation and the capture of Schumpeterian rents in disequilibrium. Both Teece (2007) and Eisenhardt and Martin (2000) propose that the pursuit of a "sustainable" competitive advantage through these ordinary capabilities needs to be relinquished in high-velocity markets, which is also a view shared by D'Aveni (1994) in the context of hypercompetitive industries. However, the Teecean view of dynamic capabilities differs quite substantially from the view of Eisenhardt and Martin (2000) and D'Aveni (1994) in that the Teecean view postulates that sustainable competitive advantage can indeed be achieved through the deployment of dynamic capabilities.

When the external environment of the firm transitions from low and medium to high and very high levels of strategic uncertainty and organizational misalignment, then profound and radical transformations to an existing strategy and its underlying business model will need to be introduced. In such cases, ordinary and dynamic capabilities collapse and dynamic metacapabilities will need to be deployed to implement the high degrees of flexibility needed not only for the execution of a myriad of different, and potentially opposed, strategies in parallel, but also for achieving the organizational alignment needed for their successful execution.

3.2 Introducing the Informational View of the Firm

Dynamic metacapabilities are not rooted in a resource-based view but rather in an informational view of the firm. According to this new view, firms are construed not as bundles of resources, as postulated by the resource-based view (Amit & Shoemaker, 1993; Mahoney & Pandian, 1992; Penrose, 1959; Wernerfelt, 1984), but rather as bundles of information. This informational view of the firm postulates that bundles of information decohere to bundles of resources, capabilities, and competencies as the strategic uncertainty and the organizational misalignment in the firm's environment decrease from very high and high levels, which are characteristic of environments subject to radical uncertainty (Kay & King, 2020), to moderate and low levels.

The informational view of the firm also postulates that the exploitation of actual resources, capabilities, and competencies, and the capture of Schumpeterian rents, can begin only after the process of decoherence of dynamic metacapabilities to dynamic capabilities has already taken place. It also recognizes the important role that the interplay between dynamic capabilities, with their blended focus on evolutionary and technical fitness, and ordinary capabilities, with their focus on technical fitness, plays in driving innovation and profiting from it (Teece, 1986, 2006, 2018a,b). This interplay is of particular importance in environments subject to market, technological, and industry disruption, which require that firms innovate constantly in the pursuit of a temporary as opposed to a sustainable competitive advantage (D'Aveni, 1994; D'Aveni, Dagnino, & Smith, 2010).

According to the informational view of the firm, the reduction of radical strategic uncertainty and organizational misalignment leads to a first boundary condition, which prompts dynamic metacapabilities to decohere first to the type of transformative dynamic capabilities described by Teece (2007, p. 1342) in the pursuit of evolutionary fitness and then to the type of dynamic capabilities described by Eisenhardt & Martin (2000, p. 1110) in the pursuit of evolutionary and technical fitness. The informational view of the firm also postulates that the further reduction of radical strategic uncertainty and organizational misalignment in the environment of the firm leads to a second boundary condition, which prompts the second type of dynamic capabilities described by Eisenhardt & Martin (2000, p. 1110) to decohere to ordinary capabilities. The transition through this second boundary condition is needed for firms to operate in moderately dynamic markets in the pursuit of technical fitness and are associated with the deployment of the type of VRIN resources, capabilities, and competencies postulated by the resource-based view of the firm (Barney, 1991; Penrose, 1959; Wernerfelt, 1984, 1995).

3.2.1 Second-order Effectiveness and Dynamic Metacapabilities

Second-order effectiveness deals with the question of what strategic objectives the firm shall pursue in parallel in the face of very high strategic uncertainty and organizational misalignment. Second-order effectiveness entails a search in a large space of "potentialities," each one of them representing a potential strategy that could be implemented through skeleton business models that are yet to be specified. The aim of second-order effectiveness is thus not exploitation but rather extensive exploration in that search space of potentialities. Dynamic metacapabilities allow firms to pursue second-order effectiveness by providing the firm with the information needed to transform its existing business model in the face of radical uncertainty and organizational misalignment (Kay & King, 2020). Dynamic metacapabilities can thus be best understood as a framework that sets the stage for the operationalization and implementation of the Teecean dynamic capabilities framework (Teece, 2007).

At the first stages of radical business model transformation through dynamic metacapabilities, the goal of the entrepreneurial firm is to achieve second-order effectiveness. To this end, new skeleton business models are explored and defined in purely informational terms. As bundles of information begin to "decohere" into actual bundles of resources, capabilities, and competencies, these skeleton business models abandon the purely informational realm and begin to be implemented through these bundles of resources, capabilities, and competencies. Decoherence thus entails a learning process requiring that information be translated into knowledge and knowledge into actual bundles of resources, capabilities, and competencies. According to the informational view of the firm we are proposing, resources, capabilities, and competencies do not emerge ex nihilo. They emerge as bundles of information begin to decohere to actual bundles of resources, capabilities, and competencies. As the process of decoherence unfolds throughout the lifecycle of dynamic metacapabilities shown in Figure 1, the decoherence of dynamic metacapabilities to dynamic capabilities results in a gradual shift of focus from second-order effectiveness, which is characterized by its focus on evolutionary fitness, to first-order effectiveness, which is characterized by a blended focus on evolutionary and technical fitness.

3.2.2 First-order Effectiveness and Dynamic Capabilities

First-order effectiveness is implemented through dynamic capabilities and deals with a fundamentally different question, namely, with the use of already instantiated bundles of resources, capabilities, and competencies for the actual implementation of a skeleton business model conveying the business logic of a new strategy chosen by the firm. While the aim of second-order effectiveness is evolutionary fitness by pursuing several, and potentially all possible, strategies in parallel, the aim of first-order effectiveness is both evolutionary and technical fitness by implementing a subset of strategies once the strategic uncertainty and organizational misalignment in the external and internal environment of the firm have been substantially reduced. First-order effectiveness has thus a hybrid focus on evolutionary fitness and technical fitness.

3.2.3 Ordinary Capabilities

As the process of decoherence continues to unfold throughout the innovation lifecycle shown in Figure 1, dynamic capabilities gradually decohere to ordinary capabilities. The aim of ordinary capabilities is technical fitness to exploit a fully operational business model that implements the logic of a new strategy. This focus on technical fitness allows firms to address the question of whether their current strategic objective is being achieved not only effectively but also efficiently through the deployment of ordinary capabilities, which can be construed as a combination of best industry practices and distinctive capabilities that can provide sources of competitive advantage.

Ordinary capabilities share some of the characteristics listed by Eisenhardt and Martin under the descriptions "traditional view of dynamic capabilities" and "reconceptualization of dynamic capabilities" (Eisenhardt & Martin, 2000, p. 1111). They can take the form of highly detailed and idiosyncratic routines that are the result of incremental process innovations introduced with the aim of gaining efficiency, which can be the source of competitive advantage and even sustainable competitive advantage in moderately dynamic markets. But they can also take the form of best industry practices, such as those resulting from the adoption of best-in-class enterprise software from leading vendors in functional areas such as finance and marketing,[14] which are not idiosyncratic and cannot provide a sustainable competitive advantage, as they are adopted by firms in an industry in order to bring to points of parity the capabilities and competencies associated with the best practices of competitors.[15]

3.2.4 The Dynamics of Decoherence and Collapse

While the decoherence of dynamic metacapabilities to dynamic capabilities and the decoherence of dynamic to ordinary capabilities unfold in a rather natural way as the strategic uncertainty of the external environment and the organizational misalignment of the internal environment of the firm decrease, the opposite process of collapse is more difficult to accomplish. This is especially the case for incumbents facing the decision of whether to transform their business models in environments ridden with strategic uncertainty and organizational misalignment (Kay & King, 2020).

Incumbents often shy away from deploying dynamic metacapabilities aimed at second-order effectiveness due to their "anticannibalization proclivities" (Teece, 2007, p. 1334). They often refuse to pursue radically different strategic options in the face of deep strategic uncertainty and tend to resist radical changes to their existing business models using defensive tactics whose overarching goal is to perfect their current business models. Such tactics often include incremental business model innovations, for example, through the introduction or adoption of best industry practices. In so doing, incumbents

[14] For example the adoption of productized enterprise software for enterprise resource planning (ERP) and customer relationship management (CRM), respectively.

[15] As they retain a partial focus on technical fitness, the dynamic capabilities described by Eisenhardt and Martin (2000) are often regarded as ordinary capabilities by strategic management scholars endorsing the Teecean view of dynamic capabilities (Teece, 2007).

often deploy some of the capabilities listed by Eisenhardt and Martin (2000, p. 1111) as a part of their "reconceptualization of dynamic capabilities."

The psychology of decision-making under risk (Kahneman & Tversky, 1979; Tversky & Kahneman, 1992) suggests that this bias toward implementing defensive tactics aimed at perfecting ordinary capabilities, as opposed to implementing business model transformations based on dynamic capabilities, is rooted in the psychophysics of loss aversion in the domain of gains (Tversky & Kahneman, 1992). In the present context, loss aversion in the domain of gains is reflected in the reluctance of incumbents in environments ridden with deep strategic uncertainty and organizational misalignment to radically transforming their business models while they "still" work. Such reluctance stems from the complex trade-offs associated with transforming business models that still operate in the domain of gains.

The resolution of these trade-offs is complex for it requires that incumbents sell a radically different strategic plan to internal and external stakeholders, secure the commitment of the management team to allocate resources for a radically different strategy, and align the entire organization for its successful execution. Empirical evidence suggests that incumbents that have managed to develop a sound strategy aimed at radically transforming their business models often fail to execute it due to a problem of organizational misalignment (Christensen, 1997; Johnson, Christensen, & Kagermann, 2008). This problem manifests itself in the failure of the management team to align the firm for the successful execution of the new strategy and is the result of the firm not having either a common vision, or the needed new complementary skills, or a set of incentives based on sharing the rewards in case of success (Carlson & Wilmot, 2006).

The frequency of decoherence and collapse increases in rapidly changing environments. Firms that operate in such environments need to deploy a number of strategies allowing them to gain the flexibility needed to cope with the trade-offs pervading processes of radical business model transformation (Christensen, 1997; Johnson, Christensen, & Kagermann, 2008). Dynamic metacapabilities are of the essence to achieve the type of second-order effectiveness that allows firms to gain the degrees of flexibility required to deal with radical uncertainty and organizational misalignment (Kay & King, 2020). Dynamic capabilities, on the other hand, are of the essence to achieve the type of first-order effectiveness that allows firms to deal with the actual implementation a radically new business model (Teece, 2007, 2010, 2016; Teece, Pisano, & Shuen, 1997). They are both key to enabling the type of entrepreneurial management needed by firms to thrive in industry sectors subject to radical industry, market, and technological disruption (Teece, 2016).

3.3 Quantum Management and the Operationalization of Dynamic Metacapabilities

Quantum management is a new management paradigm that operationalizes the dynamic metacapabilities framework described thus far. Quantum management draws upon the dynamic processes of decoherence and collapse that unfold throughout the innovation lifecycle of dynamic metacapabilities shown in Figure 1. Following the logic of this lifecycle, dynamic metacapabilities must decohere from their pure informational realm in order for radical business model transformations to unfold. The challenge for incumbents to adopt quantum management as a means to operationalize dynamic metacapabilities is the recognition of the interplay between dynamic metacapabilities, on the one hand, and dynamic and ordinary capabilities, on the other.

This interplay is governed by processes of decoherence and collapse that unfold throughout the dynamic metacapabilities lifecycle. Incumbents need to recognize when they need to deploy dynamic metacapabilities, when dynamic metacapabilities need to "decohere" to dynamic capabilities as the strategic uncertainty and organizational misalignment in the external and internal environment of the firm decrease from very high to high levels, and when dynamic capabilities need to decohere to ordinary capabilities once the strategic uncertainty and organizational misalignment decrease from high to moderate and low levels in order to render a new business model fully operational.

While the process of decoherence in quantum management operates at an informational level, the process of collapse operates at the level of bundles of resources, capabilities, and competencies. The purely informational level at which dynamic metacapabilities operate has its correlate in the informational world of subatomic particles described by quantum mechanics. The level of actual resources, capabilities, and competencies at which ordinary capabilities operate has it correlate in the classical world described by Newtonian mechanics. Dynamic capabilities find their quantum-mechanical correlate in the nebulous space where the quantum-mechanical world of subatomic particles transitions into the classical world.

4 Quantum Management

According to the standard view of decoherence theorists, the transition of the quantum to the classical world is governed in quantum mechanics by the process of quantum decoherence. Decoherence in quantum mechanics amounts to an increase in the von Neumann entropy (von Neumann, 2018) of a quantum-mechanical system. This increase in von Neumann entropy has been tied to the second law of thermodynamics and renders decoherence, in principle, irreversible. As pointed out by Zureck (2018, p. 11), however, the "irreversibility in the course of measurements" in quantum mechanics "may not only be the result of decoherence and the second law" but also the result of an "observer acquiring the data about the system and retaining a record of the outcome," which amounts to a gain in information that "can result in a decrease of the von Neumann entropy of the system," in which case "the irreversibility of measurements would not be a consequence of the second law." The gain-of-information interpretation is of central importance not only for the implementation of our dynamic metacapabilities framework but also for postulating an informational view of the firm.

4.1 The Informational View of the Firm

According to the informational view of the firm we have developed thus far, firms gain information about a "system" ridden with radical uncertainty and organizational misalignment by making "measurements." They then use the recorded information about the measurements' outcomes for the implementation of a new business model that conveys the logic of a radically new strategy. The operationalization of the dynamic metacapabilities framework will thus require the deployment of a number of strategies aimed at making such measurements and gaining and recording such information. This process of gathering intelligence information through dynamic metacapabilities can be construed as making a measurement to effectively reduce the number of potential objectives and strategies. The careful selection of such strategic objectives represents a boundary condition for dynamic metacapabilities, as the focus begins to shift gradually from pure exploration and discovery to exploitation.

As the boundaries between ordinary capabilities, dynamic capabilities, and dynamic metacapabilities are rather fuzzy, it is difficult to give a clear-cut separation between these different types of capabilities. This is reflected in the fact that some of the traditional dynamic capabilities analyzed by Eisenhardt and Martin (2000) are regarded as ordinary capabilities according to the reconceptualization of dynamic capabilities proposed by these authors. Likewise, some of the dynamic capabilities proposed by Eisenhardt & Martin (2000) in high-velocity markets may be regarded as ordinary capabilities when seen from the perspective of the dynamic capabilities proposed in the Teecean framework (Teece, 2007). A way to approach this problem is by outlining the boundary conditions that make dynamic metacapabilities decohere to dynamic capabilities and the boundary conditions that make dynamic capabilities decohere to ordinary capabilities.

4.2 Operationalizing Dynamic Metacapabilities

The operationalization of dynamic metacapabilities is essentially a problem of how to harness the full power of flexibility. Whenever firms face radical strategic uncertainty and organizational misalignment, the space of potential strategic objectives, and the strategies that firms may pursue to achieve them, increase exponentially (Kay & King, 2020). What is needed in such scenarios is the ability of the firm to first explore and pursue a potentially very large number of strategies in parallel by preserving the coherent superpositions of all possible outcomes, which would correspond to the state of the system prior to making the measurement, and then to gather intelligence information to reduce the search space by forcing the system under study to decohere. This strategy would not be aimed at implementing a fully operational business model but rather at experimenting with a potentially very large number of skeleton business models. The dynamic metacapabilities deployed to achieve this goal focus on exploration and discovery and aim at achieving second-order effectiveness.

Key to understanding how decoherence occurs in quantum management is the identification of the three-dimensional space within which the deployment of ordinary and dynamic capabilities, and dynamic metacapabilities, takes place, as shown in Figure 1. The first two axes that define this space measure the level of strategic uncertainty and organizational misalignment underpinning processes of incremental, substantial, and radical business model innovation, respectively. The third axis measures the level of flexibility at which ordinary and dynamic capabilities and dynamic metacapabilities operate. Firms deploy dynamic metacapabilities to gain information that reduces the strategic uncertainty and organizational misalignment in their external and internal environment. Instead of waiting until the strategic uncertainty and organizational misalignment have been reduced, firms can take a more proactive approach by deploying dynamic metacapabilities aimed at gaining information by forcing the underlying innovation ecosystem to decohere, at which point the operationalization of a given strategy in pursuit of a chosen strategic objective can be attempted.

Quantum management allows firms to deal with technology, industry, and market disruption in high-velocity markets while still operating in the domain of gains under the logic of a successful business model that took years, if not decades, to build and perfect (McGrath, 1997; Peng & Wang, 2000). With such an overarching goal in mind, we operationalize quantum management using a real options approach that deploys three classes of real options (Luehrman, 1988; McGrath, 1999; Miller & Modigliani, 1961). The first class introduces a set of real options that we have termed control options.

4.3 Control Options

Incumbent firms undergoing radical business model transformation have to validate a radically different business model that implements a radically different strategy, consolidate a still-emerging value creation system comprising all stakeholders of a new innovation ecosystem, and install inducement mechanisms for the rapid adoption of new offerings in either new or existing target markets. The control options determine the flow of control that governs the execution of the processes underlying each phase, and the stages within each phase, of the innovation lifecycle. Due to the inherent strategic uncertainty involved, the processes underlying business model innovation and transformation throughout that lifecycle are not serial but rather iterative. Control options are needed to implement such iterative processes.

4.3.1 Forwarding

The forwarding option is exercised to send the flow of control to the next phase, or to the next stage within a given phase, of the innovation lifecycle. This is the case whenever the information available in the environment of the firm reinforces the decisions made and confirms the innovation pathway pursued thus far by the firm.

4.3.2 Holding

The holding option is exercised whenever the execution of the activities in the current stage of a given phase of the innovation lifecycle needs to be put on hold until more information becomes available. This is the case whenever the information in the external and internal environment of the firm ceases to reinforce the decisions made so far and more information is needed to continue.

4.3.3 Backtracking

The backtracking option is exercised whenever the flow of control needs to be sent back to a given stage of a previous phase of the innovation lifecycle or to a previous stage within the current phase. This will be necessary whenever new information that becomes available in the current phase renders some of the decisions made in previous phases invalid or incorrect. In such cases, the flow of control needs to be sent back in order to revisit decisions previously made.

4.3.4 Aborting

The aborting option is exercised to terminate the execution of a process in the current stage of a given phase of the lifecycle. This option will be exercised whenever new information that becomes available in the current phase renders the further execution of the process ineffective. The exercise of this option releases resources that can be reallocated elsewhere.

4.3.5 Accelerating

The accelerating option is exercised whenever the firm needs to increase the intensity of processes of a given phase of the innovation lifecycle with the aim of gaining thrust for their execution. This is accomplished by committing and allocating more resources in order to speed up the processes at a given stage of a given phase of the innovation lifecycle. Defining critical milestones to reach the stated goals and setting tight deadlines for their completion are essential to implement this control option.

4.3.6 Decelerating

The decelerating option is exercised whenever the firm needs to reduce the intensity of processes of a given phase of the innovation lifecycle with the aim of slowing down their execution. This option is often difficult to execute because it presupposes the ability of managers to avoid their natural bias toward ineffective continuation. This bias also affects the execution of the backtracking and aborting options introduced previously.

4.3.7 The Governance of Control Options

Control options are governed and implemented by decision committees that make their decisions according to a set of decision-making criteria. These decisions can be complex as they involve multiple criteria that are often conflicting. The composition of such committees varies depending on the phase of the innovation lifecycle involved. Whereas in early phases of the lifecycle these committees deal with more strategic decisions and tend to involve the upper management of the firm, in subsequent phases the committees deal with more operational decisions and tend to involve managers of different functional areas within the firm. Control options lend themselves by their very nature to being implemented following information-theoretic approaches operationalizable using stage-gating and multicriteria group decision analysis methodologies (Cooper, 2008; Roy & Bertier, 1996; Zopounidis & Pardalos, 2010).

4.4 Directional Options

While control options allow firms to deal with deep uncertainty by controlling the flow of execution in the absence of relevant information, or as new information becomes available, another class of options that we call directional options play an even more important role in dealing with deep strategic uncertainty. These options determine the direction of search and are exercised to endow processes of exploration and discovery with increasing levels of flexibility. Directional options allow the firm to pursue several directions of search at the same time and play therefore a key role in managing innovation processes in environments ridden with radical uncertainty (Kay & King, 2020).

4.4.1 Multithreading

The multithreading option is exercised to allow the sharing of resources and capabilities for the simultaneous execution of the tasks associated with several instantiations of a single process within a given phase of the innovation lifecycle for a given strategy. An example of this option is the use of a team of product marketing managers to specify several prototypes in order to ascertain the best way to approach the solution to a set of important needs identified during the phase of incubation of the lifecycle.

4.4.2 Multiprogramming

The multiprogramming option is exercised to allow the sharing of resources and capabilities for the simultaneous execution of the tasks associated with several processes within the same phase of the innovation lifecycle for a given strategy. The multiprogramming option increases the flexibility achieved with the multithreading option by allowing different processes that occur in the same phase of the innovation lifecycle to be concurrently executed using the same bundle of resources and capabilities. An example of this option is the use of the same team of product marketing managers to carry out different stages of the phase of incubation, say, requirements specification for the implementation of a set of prototypes and the validation of a set of already-implemented prototypes with lead customers for a given strategy.

4.4.3 Multitasking

The multitasking option is exercised to share resources and capabilities for the simultaneous execution of the tasks associated with different processes across different phases of the lifecycle for a given strategy. This option increases the flexibility achieved with the multiprogramming option by allowing different processes that span different phases of the innovation lifecycle to be concurrently executed using the same bundle of resources and capabilities for a given strategy. An example of multitasking is the use of a team of engineers to develop and deliver the solutions required within the phase of development while at the same time using it to validate the technical feasibility of a prototype in the phase of incubation of the innovation lifecycle for a given strategy.

4.4.4 Multiprocessing

The multiprocessing option is exercised to allow the sharing of resources and capabilities for the simultaneous execution of the tasks associated with several different processes across different phases of the innovation lifecycle for more than one strategy. An example of this option is the use of the same team of product marketing managers to carry out different stages of the phase of incubation, say, requirements specification for the implementation of a set of prototypes, and the validation of a set of already-implemented prototypes with a group of lead customers during the phase of development for more than one strategy. This option implements a much higher degree of flexibility by allowing firms to pursue a greater number of strategies in parallel.

4.4.5 Superpositioning

The superpositioning option is exercised whenever the firm needs to take the multiprocessing option to a much higher level. This option can be implemented in different ways. For instance, a firm facing deep uncertainty regarding a set of strategies may delegate the execution of each strategy to different internal organizations, endowing each one of them with the resources and capabilities they need to execute the directional options explained so far to gain flexibility.

Inspired by the well-known superpositioning effect of quantum mechanics, the superpositioning option reaches its maximum expression when firms implement this option by forming a heterogeneous innovation ecosystem of separate organizations that already bring the resources, capabilities, and competencies needed to execute a great number of different strategies in parallel and by providing them with the incentives to execute them (Bogers, Chesbrough, & Moedas, 2018; Chesbrough, 2003, 2007, 2010; Chesbrough & Rosensbloom, 2002). The superpositioning option increases the flexibility to deal with deep strategic uncertainty and organizational misalignment. This option requires that firms first create a complex innovation ecosystem and then orchestrate the interactions of independent firms, organizations, and other stakeholders in that ecosystem to make sure that the interactions among them occur in a value-enhancing manner.

Driven by a set of different but mutually reinforcing value propositions, different stakeholders pursue different strategies in parallel on behalf of the firm. This frees the firm from having to plan and commit its owns resources and capabilities for the execution of a great number of strategies simultaneously but also exposes it to a lack of control over their execution. To the extent that a great deal of control over such innovation ecosystems is relinquished, a larger number of stakeholders can be engaged. This compounds the superpositioning effect and dramatically increases the execution power of the innovation ecosystem in time and space without involving the deployment of internal resources and capabilities, thus mimicking the quantum-mechanical superpositioning effect.

4.5 Alignment Options

In moderately dynamic markets, successful business models are implemented and improved through ordinary capabilities based on resources and capabilities that are valued, rare, inimitable and non-substitutable[16] (Barney, 1991; Penrose, 1995). In high-velocity markets, however, substantial changes to an existing business model requires that innovative firms deploy dynamic capabilities (Eisenhardt & Martin, 2000; Teece, 2007) and dynamic metacapabilities, as introduced thus far. This poses a major challenge to incumbent firms, especially if these changes are radical and need to be introduced to a hitherto successful business model. Rising to meet this challenge is particularly difficult for incumbents because they tend to continue to operate under the logic of their current business model. This creates a bias toward deploying and perfecting their ordinary capabilities while their business models still operate in the domain of gains (Kahneman & Tversky, 1979; Tversky & Kahneman, 1992).

Radical business model transformations require that incumbents deploy dynamic metacapabilities to cope with processes of creative destruction not only within the firm but also in its innovation ecosystem. This poses a tremendous challenge for incumbents in terms of aligning not only their entire firm but also the entire innovation ecosystem around it for the rapid transformation and successful implementation of new business models able to implement the logic of radically different corporate and business strategies under radical uncertainty (Johnson, Christensen, & Kagermann, 2008; Kay & King, 2020).

While control and directional options allow firms to deal with deep strategic uncertainty (Kay & King, 2020), there is another class of options that play a key role in obtaining the organizational alignment needed to execute new strategies that are numerous and often conflicting with one another. These options play a key role in allowing incumbent firms to transform business models that still operate in the domain of gains by addressing the question of how they can organizationally align their teams to execute the tasks required to radically transform a still successful business model. As the goal of this class of options

[16] Usually referred to as VRIN resources and capabilities.

is to organizationally align the firm for the execution of strategies aimed at transforming a business model that still operates in the domain of gains, we refer to them as alignment options.

Organizational alignment is much more difficult to obtain within firms executing a strategy that requires the radical transformation of a hitherto successful business model that is being disrupted. Alignment options allow incumbent firms to cope with technological, market or industry disruption. But they can also play a key role in the execution of strategies of emerging firms driving radical innovations.

4.5.1 Licensing

The licensing option allows firms to have access to third-party technologies, relieving them from having to develop them. By exercising this option, firms avoid not only the problem of having to acquire the resources, capabilities, and competencies needed to attempt an internal technology development strategy but also the need to align their teams for its successful execution.

4.5.2 Contracting

The contracting option is similar to the licensing option in that it relieves the firm from having to develop resources, capabilities, and competencies to develop and deliver technologies, products, services, and solutions. But unlike the licensing option, the exercise of a contracting option grants firms full title to such technologies, products, services, and solutions.

4.5.3 Outsourcing

The outsourcing option is similar to the contracting option in that it relieves the firm from having to acquire resources, capabilities, and competencies to develop and deliver products, services, and solutions. As in the case of the licensing option, the exercise of the outsourcing option does not grant firms title to such product and solutions, including their underlying technologies. But unlike the licensing option, the outsourcing option offers managed services that relieve firms from the need to license technologies. As a result, the outsourcing option grants firms higher degrees of flexibility but also lower degrees of control.

4.5.4 Separating

The separating option recognizes the need to separate innovation champions and their teams from the rest of the organization and is exercised if the execution of the processes underlying the phases of the innovation lifecycle are incompatible with the rest of the organization. Whenever this is the case, this option is usually undertaken during the early phases of exploration of the innovation lifecycle and is often executed by firms through intrapreneurship projects driven by independent innovation champions and their teams (Carlson & Wilmot, 2006).

4.5.5 Spinning Out

The spinning-out option takes the separating option to the next level by forming a new firm, finding a suitable innovation champion, and transferring all the existing tangible and intangible assets to the newly created firm. The innovation champion recruits an innovation team sharing the vision and bringing the complementary resources, capabilities, and competencies that are key to success and shares the rewards with the innovation team in case of success, all of which is needed for the innovation champion to organizationally align its innovation team toward the shared vision (Carlson & Wilmot, 2006).

Key to the success of innovation champions and their teams is the recognition that the strategic objective, and the strategies deployed to obtain it, rather than driven by a previously agreed-upon plan, are driven by the value proposition of the project and will thus change over time. This is one of the elements distinguishing entrepreneurial management, as advocated by the dynamic metacapabilities framework, from the management usually associated with incumbent firms, which is often predicated on a mixture of ordinary and dynamic capabilities. Besides eliminating the threat of organizational misalignment, the spinning-out option has other advantages, including the option to raise equity financing from institutional investors and venture capital firms.

4.5.6 Acquiring

The acquiring option is used to absorb resources and capabilities from a third party, usually through a purchase of proprietary technology or an asset or outright acquisition. This option is often used to enhance the strategic fit of a radically different new strategy.[17] While this option has the advantage of generating strategic alignment, it does not necessarily solve existing problems of organizational misalignment. In fact, it may lead to them, especially in cases of outright acquisitions. One way to avoid this problem is to encapsulate the acquired resources, capabilities, and competencies within a separate business unit. While this may reduce it, organizational misalignment may still persist

[17] Such as the acquisition of the handset manufacturing division of Nokia by Microsoft, which allowed Microsoft to generate strategic fit for its new strategy as provider of mobile devices and services (Lamberg et al., 2019).

and be difficult to overcome, as the need to integrate different sets of highly cospecialized assets across different business units is always a key challenge incumbents face to attain organizational alignment (Savov, 2017).

4.5.7 Divesting

The divesting option is exercised to relinquish the control over the exploration or exploitation of a given strategy. Differently from the spinning out option, the divesting option is used by firms to transfer to firms and organizations in their innovation ecosystems not only the assets but also the control that is needed to execute strategies that are not necessarily strategically aligned with the current strategy of the firm (Vuori & Huy, 2016).

4.5.8 Exiting

The exiting option is exercised to abandon the exploration or exploitation of a strategy. Differently from the option to divest, this option does not aim to transfer control over to other firms in the innovation ecosystem but rather to release resources and reassign and redistribute capabilities and competencies.

4.5.9 Entangling

The entangling option is exercised to seamlessly coordinate the activities of one or more firms or organizations in the innovation ecosystem of the firm in such a way as to allow them not only to develop a required set of highly cospecialized assets for the execution of one, or more than one, strategy but also to coevolve in a value-enhancing manner based on cospecialization economies. This option may be implemented by a strategy that grants control over such firms and organizations. One way to do this is by taking an equity position in other firms and organizations either directly or through a suitable controlling structure, such as a keiretsu (Aoki & Lennerfors, 2013).

Another strategy to implement this option is by forming an innovation ecosystem and characterizing and delivering a mutually reinforcing value proposition compelling enough for other firms and organizations in the ecosystem to behave and coevolve in a value-enhancing manner. Not involving large investments in such controlling structures, this latter strategy is more compelling, as it has the potential to entangle a larger number of firms and organizations in the innovation ecosystem of the firm. When obtained in this way, however, the entanglement is difficult to maintain, as value migration can easily erode an otherwise compelling value proposition among loosely connected firms and organizations in the innovation ecosystem.

4.5.10 Tunneling

The tunneling option is exercised to obtain the organizational alignment needed to implement one or several strategies whose execution requires not only resources, capabilities, and competencies but also a level of control that are beyond the reach of the firm. The tunneling option can be used whenever the firm lacks: (i) a shared vision of its strategic objective in the face of radical strategic uncertainty (Kay & King, 2020); (ii) the resources, capabilities, and competencies to achieve the thrust needed to execute one or more strategies in pursuit of a common strategic objective; and (iii) the shared rewards needed to align the entire firm and its innovation ecosystem toward achieving that common strategic objective (Carlson & Wilmot, 2006). Such lack of organizational alignment can happen for a number of different reasons.

The reasons for start-ups are usually the lack of resources, capabilities, and competencies and a not-yet-proven skeleton business model. The venture capital industry emerged in the 1950s in what then became known as Silicon Valley in the United States as a vehicle to remedy this problem for technology start-ups (Ferrary & Granovetter, 2009). In fact, the emergence and consolidation of the innovation networks of Silicon Valley in Northern California is a direct result of the global dominance of its venture capital industry as an industry that has proven to be difficult to replicate in other developed countries (Gompers & Lerner, 2004).

The reasons for incumbents are usually more subtle and are generally associated with lack of organizational alignment, which is a problem that is more difficult for incumbents than for start-ups to address and solve (Christensen, 1997). Incumbents are often publicly traded companies governed by boards that give higher priority to the short-term financial objectives of shareholders and prevent entrepreneurial managers, who are often the founders, from pursuing strategies that are risky and compromise short-term shareholder value maximization. This creates large "energy barriers" comprising deadlocks that prevent incumbents from executing strategies that are ridden with deep strategic uncertainty and organizational misalignment (Carlson & Wilmot, 2006; Kay & King, 2020). The tunneling option is exercised to overcome such "energy barriers."[18]

As they are often at odds with the mandate imposed upon publicly traded companies to maximize shareholder value, these strategies are often difficult for incumbents to pursue. By exercising the tunneling option, firms can leverage energy (resources, capabilities, and competencies) that lie not only within the

[18] The new grand strategy of Google under Alphabet deployed the tunneling option.

firm but also in its innovation ecosystem to gain the thrust needed to execute one or more strategies and pursue several strategic objectives in parallel. The execution of the tunneling option is not only often needed by incumbents facing the threat of radical business model disruption, or those driving disruption in existing industries,[19] but also by emerging firms that lack the resources to execute numerous strategies in parallel to cope with radical strategic uncertainty.

5 Discussion

Business model innovations introduce changes to the elements of a business model, be it the important needs of clients addressed in a given market segment, the products or services that solve these needs, the revenue and cost models used to monetize the value proposition and generate profits, the delivery model used to bring products or services to clients, or the competitive advantage used by firms to differentiate their value proposition from competitors (Boons & Lüdecke-Freund, 2013; Casadesus-Masanell & Ricart, 2010; Casadesus-Masanell & Zhu, 2013; Gambardella & McGahan, 2010; Massa, Tucci, & Afuah, 2017; Zott, Amit, & Massa, 2011). The types of business model innovation could be classified in incremental, substantial, and radical business model innovation, with the latter involving major changes to the aforementioned elements (Casadesus-Masanell & Zhu, 2013; Chesbrough, 2007; Massa, Tucci, & Afuah, 2017).

5.1 Business Model Innovation Through Ordinary Capabilities

Since incremental business model innovation does not involve substantial or radical changes to the organizational structure of the firm, nor to the components of the business model, nor to the objective or scope of the corporate strategy, this form of business model innovation is the most common one among firms and is usually associated with new features of existing products, services, or solutions or with introducing or perfecting internal processes through best industry practices to achieve operational efficiency (Eisenhardt & Martin, 2000). Incremental business model innovation is motivated by the need to respond to changing conditions in the environment on an ongoing basis and is implemented through ordinary capabilities that do not transform the existing business model in any fundamental way (Chesbrough & Rosensbloom, 2002; Doganova & Eyquem-Renault, 2009).

[19] The current strategy of Google under Alphabet shows how a tunneling option was exercised to grant the founders enough control to execute a new grand strategy aimed at entering and disrupting existing industries and creating new ones (Manjoo, 2015).

5.2 Business Model Innovation Through Dynamic Capabilities

Substantial business model innovation involves major changes to the components of the existing business model, which may include changes to the scope of the strategy, that is, to the business domain of the firm. This type of business model innovation usually involves major changes to the competitive advantage of firms and requires that they generate value propositions that are substantially better than those of their competitors based on the deployment of dynamic capabilities (Johnson, Christensen, & Kagermann, 2008). Apple is an incumbent characterized by this type of business model innovation, which is implemented using evasive tactics that push the entire industry to higher standards and force competitors to catch up with Apple's superior product innovations. By deploying best industry practices in product marketing and management, one of the dynamic capabilities proposed by Eisenhardt & Martin (2000), Apple's competitors bring to points of parity the key attributes of Apple's superior product value proposition. This shows how these lower-order dynamic capabilities can indeed be imitated.

Apple's rivalry with Samsung provides us with an excellent case showing how ordinary capabilities, with their focus on leveraging and perfecting VRIN resources and capabilities as a source of sustainable competitive advantage, can peacefully coexist with the type of dynamic capabilities set out by Eisenhardt & Martin (2000).[20] But this case also shows how the type of dynamic capabilities proposed by Teece (2007) can be instantiated and how they can peacefully coexist with the lower-order dynamic capabilities proposed by Eisenhardt & Martin (2000). Indeed, the innovation strategy of Apple is characterized by its avoidance of anticannibalization proclivities, which is proposed as one of the dynamic capabilities under the "seizing" category in the Teecean dynamic capabilities framework (Teece, 2007, p. 1334). This highlights a key aspect, namely, that the two types of dynamic capabilities can peacefully coexist within a firm and complement each other in a value-enhancing manner.

Apple deploys dynamic capabilities based on best product innovation practices, which correspond to the kind of lower-order dynamic capabilities described by Eisenhardt and Martin (2000, p. 1106) as imitable best industry practices. Yet the avoidance of anticannibalization proclivities, as a Teecean dynamic capability, cannot be created ex nihilo and presupposes the existence of a higher-order dynamic metacapability allowing Apple to redefine its

[20] Construed by these authors as being not only imitable or substitutable but also fungible and ultimately equifinal, this type of dynamic capabilities are only able to deliver a temporary competitive advantage (D'Aveni, 1994).

competitive advantage on an ongoing basis against the pressures not only of internal but also of external stakeholders (Arthur, 2012).

Considering the strategy of Apple in the mobile devices and services industry and the dynamic metacapabilities framework and its implementation through quantum management described thus far, two options stand out in the implementation of Apple's strategy, namely, the acceleration control option and the entanglement alignment option. While the acceleration option allows Apple to gain the thrust necessary in what is today its more strategic market, the entanglement option allows Apple to organizationally align its entire organization and its innovation ecosystem toward the next release of the iPhone as its flagship product following a very tight time schedule while its current release is still operating in the domain of gains. As the innovation ecosystem mounted by Apple around the Apple Store follows a garden-walled approach that privileges control over openness, the superposition directional option does not play a key role in the implementation of Apple's strategy. Apple's deployment of the acceleration and entanglement options together leads to a dynamic metacapability that is characteristic of Apple and is difficult to imitate. As opposed to dynamic capabilities in product innovation, this dynamic metacapability can hardly be regarded as imitable by competitors, which suggests that this metacapability is idiosyncratic.[21]

The fact that Apple's competitors can catch up with Apple's product innovations following different paths suggests that the lower-order dynamic capabilities of Apple around product innovation are not path dependent but rather equifinal.[22] However, the ability of Apple to cannibalize itself is a higher-order dynamic capability that can hardly be regarded as a best industry practice easily adoptable by its competitors. This rare and idiosyncratic higher-order dynamic capability, which is one of the microfoundations of the seizing dynamic capabilities proposed in the Teecean framework (Teece, 2007, p. 1334), is the key to implementing the kind of evasive tactics that are so characteristic of Apple (McCray, Gonzalez, & Darling, 2011). Such evasive tactics allow Apple to outcompete rivals such as Samsung while they are still trying to catch up with Apple's latest product innovations in the mobile devices and services industry (Arthur, 2012).

Although the dynamic capabilities proposed by Eisenhardt and Martin (2000) are concrete lower-order dynamic capabilities, they differ from the ordinary capabilities proposed by mainstream strategic management frameworks

[21] Which is in accordance with Teece's characterization of dynamic capabilities (Teece, 2007).

[22] Which matches the definition of dynamic capabilities in high-velocity markets provided by Eisenhardt and Martin (2000, p. 1111).

rooted in the resource-based view of the firm (Barney, 1991; Nelson, 1991; Penrose, 1959; Wernerfelt, 1984, 1995) in that they do not collapse in high-velocity markets and can lead to a temporary competitive advantage (D'Aveni, 1994; D'Aveni, Dagnino., & Smith, 2010). The dynamic capabilities described by Teece (2007), on other hand, correspond to higher-order capabilities that need to be instantiated based on dynamic metacapabilities. Lacking a dynamic metacapabilities framework for its operationalization, the Teecean dynamic capabilities framework has been criticized by some scholars as being rather vague and tautological and as lacking empirical grounding (Eisenhardt & Martin, 2000, p. 1106). Such critique overlooks the fact that the Teecean framework proposes higher-order capabilities that can be operationalized in a myriad of different ways. There is indeed a hitherto unexplored degree of underspecification and underrepresentation in the Teecean dynamic capabilities framework that is ultimately the result of the lack of a dynamic metacapabilities framework for its operationalization. Our goal is to set out such a first dynamic metacapabilities framework capable of providing the level of flexibility required to drive the strategy of entrepreneurial firms in environments subject to radical uncertainty and organizational misalignment (Kay & King, 2020).

5.3 The Role of Ordinary Capabilities

The case of Samsung highlights the role of ordinary capabilities. The strategy of Samsung is indeed based on strong ordinary capabilities in its supply chain, which allow the firm to compete with Apple by executing encirclement tactics. Samsung's ordinary capabilities in its supply chain, which constitute a source of competitive advantage based on resources that are rare and difficult to imitate, allow Samsung to compete with Apple by bringing to market a large number of product lines very efficiently (Cain, 2020). Deploying these strong ordinary capabilities, Samsung competes with Apple by providing a larger variety of product lines targeting all market segments at more competitive prices, including the very lucrative high-end segment in which Apple reigns supreme. Apple, on the other hand, deploys dynamic capabilities to outcompete Samsung in the high-end segment, forcing Samsung to continually imitate the substantial product innovations pioneered by Apple. However, the decisive factor of Apple's competitive strategy is not its ability to introduce substantial product innovations by deploying the lower-order dynamic capabilities proposed by Eisenhardt and Martin (2000, p. 1111) but rather its ability to continually cannibalize its current source of competitive advantage before its competitors are able to catch up.

5.4 Quantum Management and Dynamic Metacapabilities

The pursuit of second-order effectiveness by firms requires that they deploy dynamic metacapabilities to explore and discover different strategic options in parallel under the type of radical strategic uncertainty and organizational misalignment that pervades business model transformations (Kay & King, 2020). Our approach to the implementation of the dynamic metacapabilities framework set out in this contribution is a novel management paradigm that we have termed quantum management. Based on a real options approach that mimic quantum-mechanical effects, quantum management allows firms in environments ridden with deep strategic uncertainty and organizational misalignment to drive their strategy along the lifecycle of dynamic metacapabilities.

As the lifecycle of dynamic metacapabilities unfolds, firms explore and validate a myriad of strategic options through new information that becomes available in their environment. This reduces the strategic uncertainty and organizational misalignment and represents a boundary condition that forces dynamic metacapabilities to abandon the pure "informational realm" by decohering to dynamic capabilities. The transition of dynamic metacapabilities to dynamic capabilities is equivalent to making a measurement that causes the "sea of potentialities comprising all potential strategic options" to decohere to a number of instantiated strategies that can begin to be implemented through a skeleton business model. While the implementation of such skeleton business models requires dynamic capabilities, their further operationalization will ultimately require that dynamic capabilities decohere to ordinary capabilities.

The real options approach to quantum management leads to dynamic metacapabilities allowing firms to entertain a great number of strategies in parallel. As long as these dynamic metacapabilities have not yet decohered, these strategies can be maintained in a coherent state, thus allowing firms to deal with radical strategic uncertainty and organizational misalignment in high-velocity markets. As they begin to decohere throughout the dynamic metacapabilities lifecycle, the number of strategies is reduced and firms begin to replace second-order with first-order effectiveness by instantiating and executing strategies in environments where the strategic uncertainty and organizational misalignment have decreased from very high to medium levels.

5.5 Dynamic Metacapabilities and Quantum Management at Work

There are notable cases of incumbents that have embraced the type of dynamic metacapabilities, as introduced thus far in this contribution. Such cases show

how quantum management can be applied to deploy dynamic metacapabilities. One such case corresponds to the new grand strategy of Google. An analysis of Google's grand strategy under Alphabet from the perspective of the dynamic metacapabilities framework and its operationalization through quantum management reveals that Alphabet, as a conglomerate of interdependent firms, is indeed executing its new grand strategy by exercising many of the real options described in connection with quantum management.

According to CB Insights, Google's new grand strategy is based on the strategic axes shown in Table 1.[23]

Table 1 Strategic options pursued by Google under Alphabet

Strategic option	Description
Strategic option 1	Consolidate leadership in AI
Strategic option 2	Catch up in cloud services
Strategic option 3	Protect advertising business from competition
Strategic option 4	Grow computing and network infrastructure
Strategic option 5	Expand in Southeast and reenter China
Strategic option 6	Disrupt key industries (e.g. transportation and logistics)
Strategic option 7	Drive the data and AI-based agenda

The reasons why Google set the stage for the execution of its new grand strategy by creating Alphabet are shown in Table 2.

Table 2 Rationale for the creation of Alphabet

Top 3 reasons for the creation of Alphabet
1) Gain more control of the board to drive strategies ridden with radical uncertainty (Kay & King, 2020) and organizational misalignment[24]
2) Separate the "other bets,"[25] from Google's core advertising business
3) Separate the "moonshots,"[26] from Google's core advertising business

5.5.1 Alignment Options

Of all three classes of real options, the organizational alignment options played the most crucial role in the implementation of the new grand strategy

[23] See report at: https://www.cbinsights.com/research/report/google-strategy-teardown/.

[24] In his letter explaining the new structure, Larry Page explained that the restructuring of Google was needed to expand the scope of Google's strategy (Manjoo, 2015).

[25] Entrepreneurial agendas aimed at disrupting established industries not directly connected with Google's core computational advertising business.

[26] Highly speculative, early-stage business projects ridden with radical uncertainty (Kay & King, 2020).

of Google under Alphabet. In what follows, we analyze why and how Google exercised some of these alignment options.

Separating and Spinning Out

As a key step toward the execution of its new grand strategy, Google implemented the separation option as an organizational alignment option by creating Alphabet as a conglomerate of interdependent strategic business units. Google founders were not only able to separate several business units from its core computational advertising business. They also exercised the spinning out option by spinning out several business units and other entrepreneurial agendas as independent firms under Alphabet.

Tunneling

Google also implemented the tunneling option by executing a stock swap that gave the founders more control of the board. This had as an effect the delisting of Google from NASDAQ and the listing of Alphabet as the publicly traded company holding all the firms spun out of Google, including Google itself. This restructuring gave the founders the control of Alphabet's board needed to execute their grand strategy, which would have been much more difficult to obtain under Google's original corporate structure.

By exercising the tunneling option, Google's founders eliminated the great energy barrier that had precluded Google, as a publicly traded company that had led the computational advertising market since its creation in 2001, from expanding and diversifying its business in areas that were not related with its core advertising business and were considered highly speculative by shareholders. The tunneling option allowed Google's founders to send a clear message to investors, who would now need to invest in Alphabet not only to capitalize on the continued success of Google's core computational advertising business but also on the upside potential of all entrepreneurial agendas under Alphabet, many of which were not only ridden with radical strategic uncertainty (Kay & King, 2020) but also lacked the needed organizational alignment under Google.[27]

By combining the separation and spinning out options with the tunneling option, these business units and spun-out firms gained the flexibility needed to execute a variety of different strategies in parallel under strategic uncertainty. This is allowing Google to seize the opportunities associated with the strategic options shown in Table 1, each one of them showing varying degrees of radical strategic uncertainty and organizational misalignment (Kay & King,

[27] This was particularly so in the case of the "other bets" and "moonshot" projects of Google.

2020). These strategic options included the more speculative entrepreneurial agendas associated with Google's "other bets" and "moonshot" projects shown in Table 2.

The exercise of the tunneling option allowed Google to dramatically increase the "near decomposability" of its organization by spinning out strategic business units and entrepreneurial agendas and initiatives as independent firms under Alphabet without the encumbrances associated with incubating them within Google. Introduced by Simon (1962), near decomposability is a property according to which complex systems are organized in a hierarchy of components in such a way that the interactions among elements within components are more numerous than the interactions among different components. Included as one of the microfoundations of the Teecean dynamic capabilities framework (Teece, 2007), near decomposability reduces the complexity associated with processes of radical business model transformation and accelerates their execution.

By exercising the tunneling option Google's founders cut a long-standing Gordian knot that had prevented them from executing their new grand strategy. As a publicly traded company with its core business in the search engine marketing industry, Google's new grand strategy did face a big energy barrier. The exercise of the tunneling option did allow Google to overcome an otherwise unsurmountable energy barrier. It also provided a paradigmatic case of a successful deployment of this alignment option for the execution of strategies ridden with radical uncertainty and organizational misalignment.

Acquiring

As part of its new grand strategy, Alphabet is also exercising the acquiring option in key areas. With over 240 acquisitions that include previous acquisitions such as Motorola Mobile, Google's largest acquisition to date, Waze, the mapping service start-up based in Tel Aviv, and YouTube, the video sharing platform,[28] Google's exercise of the acquiring option is not new and includes Android as its most important acquisition to date (Callaham, 2018).

As part of its new grand strategy, Alphabet continues to drive acquisitions that are aligned with the strategic options shown in Table 1. They include the recent creation of Google DeepMind, a firm that resulted from the merger of Google Brain, the deep learning lab at Google, with DeepMind, the UK-based machine learning start-up that had been acquired by Google in 2014. Positioned as one of the world's leading deep learning R&D labs (Roth & Peter, 2023), Google DeepMind contributes to the execution of the first strategic option

[28] See: www.cbinsights.com/research/google-biggest-acquisitions-infographic/.

shown in Table 1, namely, to consolidate its leadership in Artificial Intelligence as the general-purpose technology platform of the Industry 4.0 and beyond. This option has also been exercised to include acquisitions that are aligned with the second strategic option shown in Table 1, namely, to catch up in cloud services, such as the recent acquisition of Mandiant, a leading firm in the area of cybersecurity.[29]

Entangling

As a result of exercising the three options described previously, Google's founders effectively created an extended innovation ecosystem. As part of the governance of this newly formed innovation ecosystem, Google needed a governance mechanism able to master a hard balancing act between granting the firms and organizations in this innovation ecosystem a great deal of independence while at the same time allowing the founders to exert control over them through Alphabet. To this end, the strategy of the independent firms that resulted from the exercise of the tunneling, spinning-out, and acquiring options discussed previously needed to be orchestrated so as to exploit synergetic potentials among them in a value-enhancing way. This was accomplished by exercising the entangling option and by implementing it based on key entangling principles.

The implementation of this option in the case of Google was achieved by entangling the firms under Alphabet through principles stipulated and orchestrated by Alphabet as the overarching corporate structure. In this particular implementation, Alphabet orchestrates the execution of its overall grand strategy, making sure that the independent strategies pursued by each of the firms under Alphabet are guided by key entangling principles that include: (i) leading the development of general general-purpose technology platforms such as Artificial Intelligence and quantum computing; (ii) sustaining Google's global dominance in the computational advertising market; and (iii) increasing Google's competitiveness in the global cloud services industry so as to catch up with Amazon Web Services and Microsoft Azure, the two companies that still dominate this industry.

5.5.2 Directional Options

The new grand strategy of Google has also been implemented through the exercise of directional options, as described next.

[29] See acquisition details online at: https://cloud.google.com/blog/products/identity-security/google-completes-acquisition-of-mandiant.

Superpositioning

The radical strategic uncertainty and organizational misalignment associated with the new grand strategy of Google required that different strategies be executed in parallel without any of the encumbrances and burdens of Google as a publicly traded firm and leader in computational advertising. Achieving this goal required the exercise of the superpositioning option. Google implemented this option by forming a very heterogeneous ecosystem of firms under Alphabet, endowing them with the resources and capabilities needed to execute a large number of strategies in parallel to deal with radical strategic uncertainty (Kay & King, 2020). The superpositioning option, combined with some of the alignment options discussed previously, allowed Alphabet to endow the firms and business units in its innovation ecosystem with innovation champions and innovation teams with a common vision, shared rewards, and the complementary skills needed to overcome the problems of organizational misalignment that would have otherwise arisen had these strategies been executed within Google as incumbent in the computational advertising industry (Carlson & Wilmot, 2006).

The superpositioning option allowed Alphabet to pursue different strategies in parallel, including innovation strategies aimed at sustaining the competitiveness of Google's core computational advertising business, which had long entered the phase of exploitation and focused on technical fitness and the capture of Schumpeterian rents. But they also included other innovation strategies that were still in the incubation phase of exploration and discovery and were aimed at generating evolutionary fitness. These superposed strategies included more speculative innovation strategies such as those associated with the "other bets" and the "moonshot" projects listed in Table 2. The strategies aimed at sustaining the competitiveness of Google's core computational advertising business were consistent with the goals and expectations of shareholders and potential investors and did not necessarily require a corporate restructuring. But the strategies associated with the "other bets" and the "moonshots" projects of Google did conflict with these goals and expectations. In fact, the lack of strategic and organizational alignment would have rendered the planning and commitment of resources for the execution of these more speculative projects much more difficult to approve by the board of directors.

The exercise of the superpositioning option as part of the new grand strategy of Google was of highly strategic importance. It allowed Google's founders as "entrepreneurial managers" to gain the flexibility needed to pursue their grand vision of Google as a diversified conglomerate entering and disrupting industry sectors still dominated by firms with conventional pipeline business models (van Alstyne, Parker, & Choudary, 2016).[30] Transforming this great vision into reality required the execution of a myriad of strategies in parallel, many of them pursuing rather conflicting objectives. They included strategies aimed at protecting Google's core computational advertising business from the threat posed by competitors and new entrants but also more speculative projects that had a high upside potential but were ridden with higher degrees of radical strategic uncertainty and organizational misalignment.

Multiprocessing

The recent announcement of Demis Hassabis, DeepMind's CEO, to launch Google DeepMind as the new unit within Google that unites the teams of Google Brain, the research unit of Google Research in the area of deep learning, and DeepMind, the UK-based machine learning start-up acquired by Google in 2014, is an example of the multiprocessing option (Roth & Peter, 2023). This directional option is exercised to share resources and capabilities for the execution of the tasks associated with different processes across different stages and phases of the innovation lifecycle for a potentially large number of different strategies. According to Hassabis,[31] the new Google DeepMind unit can be leveraged by other Google product areas for the execution of different product innovation and development strategies.[32]

5.5.3 Control Options

The new grand strategy of Google has also been implemented through the exercise of control options, as described next.

Accelerating

Of all the control options described under the first class of real options, the most salient one in the case of the new grand strategy of Google under Alphabet is the accelerating option. The exercise of this option endowed the independent firms under Alphabet with the resources needed to speed up the execution of their strategies. This was accomplished by positioning Alphabet as the publicly traded company under which most of the firms driving intrapreneurial agendas not directly part of the core business of Google were held. This endowed Alphabet with the liquidity, and Google's founders with the control, needed to plan and commit the resources needed to accelerate the execution of the different strategies pursued by the firms under Alphabet. Google's exercise of

---

[30] These are conventional brick-and-mortar or click-and-mortar businesses that operate in linear value chains as opposed to value creation systems (Normann, 2001).

[31] See announcement at: www.deepmind.com/blog/announcing-google-deepmind.

[32] Which can also be leveraged by other product areas within other firms under Alphabet.

this option is also a good example of the interplay between the real options introduced under the three classes of real options described in connection with quantum management and the informational view of the firm.

By exercising the tunneling option as an alignment option, Alphabet gained the liquidity required, and Google's founders the power to exercise the accelerating option as a control option. The exercise of this accelerating option allowed Google's founders to speed up the execution of all the strategies pursued by the firms under Alphabet, which had been instantiated through the exercise of the superpositioning option, a directional option that had allowed Alphabet to execute a myriad of strategies in parallel. The end result is the accelerated execution of a variety of strategies for all independent firms under Alphabet simultaneously, including the strategies of the "other bets" and the "moonshot" projects of Google, which had been difficult to justify, let alone commit to, under the corporate veil of Google as a publicly traded firm.

Aborting

The exercise of the aborting control option is common in innovation projects and Google is certainly no exception. Although not directly related to the grand new strategy of Google under Alphabet, Google+, the answer of Google to Facebook, is perhaps the most notorious application to be aborted by Google, which in this particular case was mainly due to lack of user engagement (Welch, 2019). At a rather corporate level, the exercise of the aborting option by abandoning the strategy of positioning Google as the incumbent search engine in the Chinese market in 2010 was due to a lack of organizational alignment with key external stakeholders of the local innovation ecosystem in China prior to the emergence of the Chinese data-industrial complex (Sheehan, 2018).

5.6 Dynamic Capabilities and Dynamic Metacapabilities

The grand new strategy of Google under Alphabet is an excellent case of how dynamic capabilities and dynamic metacapabilities can peacefully coexist. Some of the strategic options listed in Table 2 are associated with businesses with a fully functional business model that had implemented a strategy based on the deployment of dynamic and ordinary capabilities and was already delivering Schumpeterian rents. These include businesses in which Google has positioned itself as the incumbent, such as its core computational advertising business, and those in which Google has been forced to catch up as late entrant, such as the global cloud services business. But Google's entrepreneurial agendas also include the "other bets," which are radical innovation agendas aimed at reshaping large mature industries, such as transportation and healthcare, by rendering the current business models of incumbents in these industries obsolete.

Most industries are still dominated by incumbents operating under the logic of conventional "pipeline" business models in which the value creation process takes place in linear value chains (van Alstyne, Parker, & Choudary, 2016). Despite ongoing efforts to transform their brick-and-mortar business models into click-and-mortar business models through digital transformation, incumbents in these industries are having a hard time trying to transform their pipeline business models into digital platform business models. As pointed out by Parker, van Alstyne, and Choudary (2016), the challenge for incumbents lies in that adding digital platform functionality to a conventional business model is much harder than adding product and service functionality to a platform business model. As a result, Google's "other bets" threaten to disrupt incumbents in mature industries by invading their space with digital platform business models that outcompete their pipeline business models and are poised to become the business models of the Internet of Things as the transportation infrastructure of the Industry 4.0 and beyond.

But the business strategy of Google's "other bets" is still mostly characterized by a lack of a functional business model able to capture Schumpeterian rents. From an information theory standpoint (Shannon, 1948), this lack of functionality lies in the lack of actionable information in the face of radical strategic uncertainty (Kay & King, 2020), which causes the collapse of dynamic capabilities and forces the deployment of dynamic metacapabilities aimed at gaining information in the pursuit of second-order effectiveness and evolutionary fitness. Other entrepreneurial agendas that Google is pursuing through the deployment of dynamic metacapabilities include businesses that are yet to emerge as viable and where Google does not yet have a skeleton business model, such as Google's moonshot projects.

The new grand strategy of Google is not only a quintessential case of dynamic metacapabilities at work but also of peaceful coexistence of ordinary and dynamic capabilities, on the one hand, and dynamic metacapabilities, on the other. Although this is by no means an isolated case, the cases of incumbents that led an industry and failed to transform their business models in the face of market, industry, and technological disruption are definitely more numerous (Christensen, 1997). These cases reveal the need to understand what dynamic metacapabilities are and when and how to deploy them. We hope the dynamic metacapabilities framework we have introduced in this contribution will be a first step toward filling this important gap.

6 Conclusions

We conclude by analyzing the contributions of the dynamic metacapabilities framework and the informational view of the firm.

6.1 Integrating Dynamic Capabilities into Evolutionary Economics

As advocated in a recent contribution by Teece (2023), the disconnect between the notion of dynamic capabilities, as understood in strategic management, and the notion of routines, as understood in evolutionary economics, is in part due to the absence of the role of what Teece (2023, p. 206) refers to as "entrepreneurial management" in enabling "evolution with design, purpose, and strategy." This conceptualization of firm evolution challenges its generally accepted view in evolutionary economics, which construes firm evolution as a process that unfolds in a bottom-up fashion without recourse to any top-down design, purpose, or strategy. Yet the current disconnect around the very concept of dynamic capabilities is not only due to the different views on firm evolution held by strategic management scholars and evolutionary economists. We argue that the main reason for this disconnect is more profound and lies in the lack of an operationalization of dynamic capabilities in strategic management.

The objective of the dynamic capabilities framework is to allow firms to adopt and "implement" entrepreneurial management in rapidly changing environments subject to radical uncertainty and organizational misalignment (Teece, 2016). Although a set of microfoundations of dynamic capabilities have been proposed (Teece, 2007), they not only lack a formal operationalization but have also remained underspecified. Despite a comprehensive body of work since the 1990s, an operationalization of "entrepreneurial management," that is, an operationalization of dynamic capabilities, has proven to be a tough nut to crack in the field of strategic management. Given their endorsement of the top-down view of firm evolution, such lack of operationalization is more surprising among strategic management scholars, especially those advocating the Teecean view of dynamic capabilities and the role of entrepreneurial managers in firm evolution, than among evolutionary economists. Lacking such operationalization, entrepreneurial management has not only remained a nebulous and elusive concept among strategic management scholars and evolutionary economists. More importantly from a managerial standpoint, it has also remained difficult to implement and execute by (entrepreneurial) managers.

One of our main contributions at the intersection of strategic management and evolutionary economics thus lies in the operationalization of this form of entrepreneurial management. Based on three classes of real options that mimic quantum-mechanical effects, we call this new management paradigm "quantum management." The three classes of real options introduced thus far are an important step toward the operationalization of quantum management based on an informational view of the firm. However, the goal of quantum management is not only theoretical by bringing firm evolution "with design, purpose, and strategy" into evolutionary economics, as recently advocated by Teece (2023). Quantum management has also important practical implications.

Operationalized through control, directional, and alignment options, quantum management sets out a decision-theoretic framework able to guide not only incumbents but also emerging firms in their pursuit of radical business model transformations along what we have referred to as the lifecycle of dynamic metacapabilities in environments dominated by deep strategic uncertainty and organizational misalignment (Kay & King, 2020). While this lifecycle approach allows us to model the dynamics of business model transformation over time, the real options approach to quantum management provides the flexibility required to deal with deep strategic uncertainty and overcome the problems of organizational misalignment that pervade business model transformations.

6.2 Quantum Management: From Dynamic Metacapabilities to Dynamic and Ordinary Capabilities

As opposed to the dynamic capabilities described by Eisenhardt and Martin (2000) with its focus on incremental and substantial business model innovation through the adoption of best industry practices, dynamic metacapabilities aim to implement the high degrees of flexibility needed to manage processes of business model transformation under radical strategic uncertainty and organizational misalignment (Kay & King, 2020). Dynamic metacapabilities also differ from the dynamic capabilities described by Teece (2007) in that they correspond to a framework of metacapabilities that can be deployed to gain the information needed to implement some of the microfoundations of the Teecean dynamic capabilities framework (Teece, 2007) in environments ridden with high levels of strategic uncertainty and organizational misalignment.

The lifecycle approach to dynamic metacapabilities we follow proposes a continuum from dynamic metacapabilities to dynamic capabilities and ultimately to ordinary capabilities as well as the existence of boundary conditions for the collapse of ordinary to dynamic capabilities, and the collapse of dynamic capabilities to dynamic metacapabilities. It also proposes boundary conditions for the inverse process of decoherence of dynamic metacapabilities to dynamic capabilities, and the decoherence of dynamic capabilities to ordinary capabilities. Inspired by quantum mechanics, decoherence occurs as processes of exploration and discovery lead to new information[33] that reduces the

[33] Which in quantum mechanics corresponds to making a measurement and recording its value.

strategic uncertainty and organizational misalignment in the external and internal environment of the firm. This focus on information as the primordial asset that will lead to resources and capabilities in subsequent phases of the dynamic metacapabilities lifecycle leads to an informational view of the firm.

According to this new informational view, resources and capabilities are not created ex nihilo but are rather the result of processes of decoherence that take place as business model transformations unfold throughout the different phases of the dynamic metacapabilities lifecycle. Given the focus of dynamic metacapabilities on evolutionary fitness, we have operationalized the dynamic metacapabilities framework through a novel management paradigm that we call quantum management. By integrating the lifecycle approach to dynamic metacapabilities with a real options approach that mimics quantum-mechanical effects, quantum management allows us to unleash the power of real options in terms of increasing not only the variety of strategic options available to the firm in the face of radical strategic uncertainty and organizational misalignment but also the flexibility to entertain them as "potential strategic options" so long as the "coherence" among them is preserved[34] and dynamic metacapabilities have not yet "decohered" to actual bundles of dynamic capabilities.[35]

While the metacapabilities lifecycle approach allows managers to deploy decision-theoretic frameworks able to guide them in the complex decisions of collapse and decoherence that pervade the type of entrepreneurial management proposed by Teece (2016), the real options approach to quantum management we follow allows (quantum) managers to implement the high levels of flexibility needed to deal with the kind of radical strategic uncertainty and organizational misalignment that is inherent to business model transformations in environments subject to frequent technological, market, and industry disruption.

6.3 Toward an Informational Theory of the Firm

The dynamic metacapabilities framework and its operationalization through quantum management is quite a departure from mainstream strategic

---

[34] Coherence is preserved so long as these strategic options remain in the informational realm, that is, so long as they remain in a coherent state that preserves their superposition.

[35] While in quantum mechanics decoherence is generally considered irreversible through a gain of information that forces a quantum-mechanical system to lose coherent states, in quantum management decoherence is in general reversible through the opposite process of loss of information. As a result of a loss of information caused by an increase in the strategic uncertainty and organizational misalignment in the environment of the firm, dynamic capabilities collapse to dynamic metacapabilities, allowing the firm to entertain new bundles of potential strategic options that peacefully coexist in a coherent state of superposition.

management frameworks, including dynamic capabilities frameworks based on the resource-based view of the firm (Barney, 1991; Penrose, 1995).

Ordinary capabilities are construed as "VRIN capabilities" that provide sources of a sustainable competitive advantage (Wernerfelt, 1984, p. 1344). Eisenhardt & Martin (2000, p. 1111) construe dynamic capabilities as "best industry practices that are imitable, fungible and equifinal" and can thus provide sources of a competitive advantage that is not sustainable but rather temporary. Teece (2007, p. 1319) construes dynamic capabilities as those "necessary to sustain superior enterprise performance in an open economy with rapid innovation and globally dispersed sources of invention, innovation, and manufacturing." These three frameworks are all rooted in the resource-based view as one of the most mainstream theories of the firm (Barney, 1991; Penrose, 1995; Wernerfelt, 1984) and inherit one of the main implicit assumptions of this view, namely, that resources and capabilities are created ex nihilo and are therefore elemental.

Based on an informational view of the firm, the dynamic metacapabilities framework is quite a departure from all these strategic management frameworks rooted in the resource-based view of the firm in that it does not construe ordinary and dynamic capabilities as emerging ex nihilo (Barney, 1991; Penrose, 1995). Operationalized through quantum management, dynamic metacapabilities operate in an informational space, that is, they subsume all capabilities only as potentialities that have yet to materialize. To give rise to dynamic and ultimately to ordinary capabilities, dynamic metacapabilities will have to "decohere" from the pure informational realm of potentialities to knowledge and ultimately to actual bundles of capabilities as the process of "decoherence"[36] unfolds throughout the lifecycle of dynamic metacapabilities.

As mentioned, the dynamic metacapabilities framework we are proposing construes neither ordinary nor dynamic capabilities as emerging ex nihilo. Furthermore, as knowledge derives from information and cannot be considered elemental (Devlin, 1999), the dynamic metacapabilities framework construes neither ordinary nor dynamic capabilities as emerging from knowledge recombinations either.[37] According to the informational view of the firm we are proposing, while knowledge emerges if new valuable uses can be discovered for new information, new information emerges by harvesting data via exploration and discovery (Devlin, 1999), which in quantum-mechanical terms corresponds to making a measurement and keeping a record of it. Thus, in the

[36] Which is a process that entails losing coherent states of superposition via gains of information.

[37] As suggested by some strategic management scholars, who have recognized knowledge resources as an important factor in high-velocity markets (Grant, 1996; Kogut, 1996).

final analysis, ordinary and dynamic capabilities neither emerge ex nihilo nor emerge from knowledge recombinations. They emerge as a result of deploying bundles of dynamic metacapabilities that operate at a higher-order, purely informational level and are implemented through quantum management following a real options approach.

The dynamic metacapabilities framework we have set out in this contribution assumes that knowledge, resources, and ultimately capabilities, whether ordinary or dynamic, are the result of bundles of information decohering to actual bundles of resources and capabilities as the strategic uncertainty and organizational misalignment in the external and internal environment of the firm decrease from very high levels to moderate and low levels (Eisenhardt & Martin, 2000; Kay & King, 2020). Operationalized through quantum management, the dynamic metacapabilities framework thus adopts a much more fundamental informational view, as opposed to a knowledge- or resource-based view, of the firm. We call it the "informational view of the firm."

We argue that the informational view of the firm adopted by the dynamic metacapabilities framework and operationalized through quantum management is of the essence to implement the kind of entrepreneurial management advocated by the Teecean framework of dynamic capabilities (Teece, 2007). Given its operationalization through three classes of real options that mimic quantum-mechanical effects, we have chosen the term "quantum management" for our implementation of this type of entrepreneurial management (Teece, 2016).

The parallel between quantum mechanics and dynamic metacapabilities, on the one hand, and classical mechanics and the capabilities advocated by the resourced based view of the firm, on the other, is in part motivated by the need to drop the assumption that ordinary capabilities are generated ex nihilo. As mentioned previously, the informational view of the firm postulates that capabilities are not generated ex nihilo but are rather the result of bundles of information "decohering" to actual capabilities, whether dynamic or ordinary, as new information becomes available to the firm. Such gain of information reduces the radical uncertainty and prompts the firm to instantiate new dynamic capabilities in high-velocity markets and rapidly changing environments, which are then perfected into ordinary capabilities that can then be deployed in the pursuit of technical fitness whenever the radical uncertainty and organizational misalignment have been substantially reduced.

From a theoretical standpoint, we think that drawing this parallel between quantum mechanics and dynamic metacapabilities is not only valid but also very helpful because it allows us to understand how the informational realm in which dynamic metacapabilities operate differs from the realm of actual capabilities, whether dynamic or ordinary, in which a firm operates whenever the radical uncertainly and organizational misalignment in its environment have been reduced from very high levels to moderate and low levels. Just as quantum mechanics describes subatomic particles not in terms of actual objects but rather in terms of information about not-yet-materialized potential objects, the dynamic metacapabilities framework describes capabilities not in terms of actual capabilities but rather in terms of bundles of information about not-yet-materialized potential capabilities. These bundles of information have only the potential to become actual capabilities as the process of decoherence unfolds throughout the lifecycle of dynamic metacapabilities.

Borrowed from quantum mechanics, the gains of information associated with decoherence reduce the strategic uncertainty and organizational misalignment in the environment of the firm (Kay & King, 2020) and are of the essence for the instantiation of actual dynamic and ordinary capabilities.

6.3.1 Quantum Management and the Informational View of the Firm

The deployment of the three classes of real options we are proposing is a natural way to operationalize the dynamic metacapabilities framework. As pointed out by Kogut & Kulatikala (2001), strategy under uncertainty can be construed as a portfolio of real options allowing firms to implement flexibility in rapidly changing and unpredictable environments. While real options approaches have been used in the past to harness the power of flexibility and deal with uncertainty (Kogut & Kulatikala, 2001; Kogut & Kulatilaka, 1994; Luehrman, 1988; McGrath, 1997, 1999), the three classes of real options we have introduced, namely, control, directional and alignment options, are a novel development.

Previous approaches to strategy based on real options allow firms to apply heuristics to implement strategy under uncertainty (Bowman & Moskowitz, 2001; Kogut & Kulatikala, 2001; Trigeorgis & Reuer, 2017). By mimicking quantum-mechanical effects, however, the real options approach we follow for operationalizing dynamic metacapabilities allows firms to deploy metaheuristics to implement strategy in environments ridden with high levels of uncertainty and organizational misalignment.

Operationalized by real options that can be deployed either in stand-alone mode or in combination, the resulting dynamic metacapabilities framework benefits from deploying an array of metaheuristics that mimic well-known quantum-mechanical effects under radical uncertainty (Kay & King, 2020). In our view, this is not only a novel but also a strong point that has found application in other disciplines already.

Consider for example the superposition effect of quantum mechanics. In quantum biology, this effect would provide a plausible explanation for how the solar energy contained in a photon can be converted into electrochemical energy in the "reactor center" located in the cells of the plants' leaves with almost 100 percent quantum efficiency, which is a question that has puzzled biologists for decades. Although research in quantum biology suggesting that quantum-mechanical effects are at play in the highly efficient process of photosynthesis is still ongoing, the research findings so far have led quantum biologists to propose the so-called quantum design of photosynthesis as a highly efficient model for the design of bio-inspired solar energy conversion systems (Romero, Novoderezhkin, & van Grondelle, 2017).

Similarly, the implementation of the superpositioning option as a directional option allows firms to pursue a potentially very large number of strategic options in parallel, often using resources and capabilities that are owned and controlled not by them but rather by other interested parties in their innovation ecosystems. Firms able to deploy this directional option can dramatically increase their effectiveness in environments subject to deep strategic uncertainty while at the same time increasing their efficiency by reducing "energy dissipation" through the use of resources and capabilities that lie outside the firm.

6.3.2 Dynamic Metacapabilities and the Social Sciences

The dynamic metacapabilities framework and its operationalization through quantum management have important implications in the social sciences. Dynamic metacapabilities facilitate entrepreneurial management at the microlevel of firms, allowing entrepreneurial managers to replace the logic of leveraging core capabilities as sources of competitive advantage, which is rooted in the resource-based view of the firm (Barney, 1991; Penrose, 1995; Wernerfelt, 1984), with the logic of opportunity and change (Eisenhardt & Martin, 2000; Teece, 2007). They also play an important role not only at the mesolevel of innovation networks by positioning firms as "orchestrators" of complex innovation ecosystems but also at the macrolevel of technological innovation systems by driving innovation in industry sectors subject to rapid technological, market, and industry disruption.

While we have focused so far on the application of dynamic metacapabilities in economics and management, we argue that other areas in the social sciences dealing with hard decision-making problems in complex social systems subject to deep strategic uncertainty and organizational misalignment can benefit from the application of dynamic metacapabilities as well.

6.3.3 The Transition from Dynamic Metacapabilities to Dynamic and Ordinary Capabilities

The transition from quantum to classical mechanics, as theories that aim to describe the physical world, occurs when we leave the informational realm of subatomic particles described by quantum mechanics and enter the material realm of macroscopic objects described by classical mechanics. Similarly, the transition from an informational view of the firm based on dynamic metacapabilities to a resource-based view of the firm based on dynamic capabilities and ordinary capabilities occurs whenever the need to implement very high and high levels of flexibility subsides. According to the dynamic metacapabilities framework, this occurs whenever firms reduce the strategic uncertainty and organizational misalignment in their internal and external environment through gains of information as the process of decoherence unfolds throughout the lifecycle of dynamic metacapabilities.

Quantum management, as a working paradigm chosen to implement the kind of entrepreneurial management needed by firms in environments ridden with high strategic uncertainty and organizational misalignment, has several advantages. Chief among them is that quantum management allows firms to implement strategies that harness the power of very high levels of flexibility in the face of very high levels of strategic uncertainty and organizational misalignment by mimicking quantum-mechanical effects as metaheuristics. Another advantage is that metaheuristics do not need to reproduce quantum-mechanical effects in a physical or biological system. Implemented through bundles of control, directional, and alignment options that "mimic" quantum-mechanical effects, firms can take advantage of these effects while at the same time ridding themselves of the need to avoid decoherence.

Decoherence poses indeed a major challenge when it comes to replicating and benefiting from quantum-mechanical effects in other application domains. Consider, for example, the current quest for quantum computing as the new computing paradigm that will leave digital computing as a relic of the past. Preserving quantum-mechanical effects by avoiding decoherence of the underlying physical components of the quantum computing device is a major stumbling block toward the implementation of the first commercial-grade quantum computers. Quantum biology has also emerged as new field in biology that aims to understand how quantum mechanical effects play a major role in key biological phenomena such as photosynthesis and gene mutation, to name but a few, which seem to suggest that biological systems may indeed have found a way to avoid decoherence to preserve quantum mechanical effects through processes that are not yet well understood (Romero, Novoderezhkin, & van Grondelle, 2017).

Decoherence in the dynamic metacapabilities framework does not occur as an undesirable process that destroys coherent states and leads to losing the desired quantum mechanical effects in a quantum-mechanical system but rather as a controlled process that unfolds as a result of gains of information that reduce the strategic uncertainty and organizational misalignment in the environment of the firm. Unlike decoherence in a quantum-mechanical system, decoherence in the dynamic metacapabilities framework can be reversed as a result of an increase in the strategic uncertainty and organizational misalignment in the environment of the firm from low and moderate levels to high and very high levels. The reversibility of decoherence in the dynamic metacapabilities framework manifests itself in the process of collapse shown in Figure 1.

6.3.4 Deploying Dynamic Metacapabilities, Bounded Rationality, and Cognitive Costs

Firms deploying dynamic metacapabilities need to assume not only bounded rationality on the part of their managers (Kahneman & Tversky, 1979; Tversky & Kahneman, 1992) but also an increase in cognitive costs (Loasby, 1967, 1990). Increased cognitive costs limit the ability of firms to grow (Penrose, 1959) and impose a constraint on firm growth that has been referred to as the "Penrose effect." Despite scholarly work on how to overcome the cognitive constraints associated with managerial decision-making in growing firms (Hay & Morris, 1991), the question arises as to how "quantum managers" can cope with the increasing cognitive costs of deploying dynamic metacapabilities.

As already explained throughout this contribution, a firm deploying dynamic metacapabilities can benefit from mimicking quantum-mechanical effects through bundles of control, directional, and alignment options. This results in leveraging resources and capabilities that are owned and controlled not by the firm but rather by interested parties in its innovation ecosystem. In so doing, the lion's share of cognitive costs can be transferred by the firm to external interested parties. This dramatically reduces the cognitive costs of the firm, which can then assume the role of "orchestrator" of the different strategies being pursued and entertained by different interested parties in its innovation ecosystem. The end result is a gain in efficiency by dramatically reducing the cognitive costs assumed by the firm. But this gain comes at the price of losing total control over the execution of multiple strategies in parallel.

One way for firms deploying dynamic metacapabilities to address the potential threat of losing control is to share with interested parties complementary assets that are needed for the execution of these strategies while still maintaining ownership and control over them. Another way for firms to keep this threat at bay is to implement more complex governance models of the innovation ecosystems they orchestrate based on overarching principles of "coopetition."

6.4 Dynamic Metacapabilities as a Normative Framework

Dynamic metacapabilities constitute a normative framework in that it proposes a number of metaheuristics for firms to "evolve with purpose and strategy" (Teece, 2023, p. 215) in environments ridden with radical uncertainty and organizational misalignment. But it is also a framework grounded on cases of success and failure in driving and executing strategy in environments subject to technological, industrial, and market disruption. While cases of incumbent firms that failed to transform their business models in the face of technological, industrial, and market disruption abound (Christensen, 1997),[38] cases of firms that have successfully implemented dynamic metacapabilities are not uncommon. The new grand strategy of Google under Alphabet is a quintessential example of dynamic metacapabilities at work. Other cases of incumbent firms that have already applied dynamic metacapabilities successfully include the rise of the of online ad syndication industry led by Google in 2002, the case of Twitter in its quest for a revenue model after its successful IPO in 2013, and the catch-up strategy of Google with Apple in 2010 (Paredes-Frigolett & Pyka, 2023).

The Industry 4.0, as the first data-driven industrial revolution, is already exacerbating the level of technological, industrial, and market disruption in several industry sectors. Incumbents in almost any industry sector are currently struggling with the problem of transforming their current click-and-mortar business models to data-driven platforms business models. The current adoption of Artificial Intelligence and future adoption of Artificial General Intelligence as the general-purpose technology platform of the Industry 4.0 and beyond will exacerbate the level of disruption going forward.

Firms that still operate today under the logic of conventional pipeline business models rooted in the resource-based view of the firm (Barney, 1991; Penrose, 1995; Wernerfelt, 1984) will need to deploy dynamic metacapabilities to achieve very high levels of flexibility in the face of very high levels of strategic uncertainty and organizational misalignment in their internal and

[38] The most notorious cases being those of Kodak and Nokia (Anthony, 2016; Lamberg et al., 2019; McCray, Gonzalez, & Darling, 2011; Shih, 2016; Vuori & Huy, 2016).

external environment with the ultimate goal of radically transforming their business models. These ongoing developments will contribute to consolidating the informational view of the firm we have set out in this contribution.

6.5 Dynamic Metacapabilities, the Informational View of the Firm, and How Firms Come into Existence

Both frameworks, the informational view of the firm we are advocating, on the one hand, and the resourced-based view of the firm, as a mainstream theory of the firm in strategic management and evolutionary economics, on the other, aim to explain why firms exist and how they come into existence and grow. The answer to the all-important question of how firms come into existence, however, differs in these two views of the firm in a very fundamental way.

According to the resource-based view of the firm, the answer to this question lies in the concept of core resources and capabilities that are valuable, rare, inimitable, and non-substitutable and are thus a source of sustainable competitive advantage. The informational view of the firm we are proposing differs from this resource-based view of the firm in that the genesis of the firm does not begin with the instantiation of core resources and capabilities, as defined previously, nor with the instantiation of core resources and capabilities aimed at exploring investments to deal with future threats or seize future opportunities.[39] The informational view of the firm considers that the answer to the question of how firms come into existence lies in information as a precursor of knowledge, resources, capabilities, and competencies.

Information differs from knowledge, resources, capabilities, and also competencies in a very fundamental way. Resources presuppose the existence of assets and knowledge about valuable uses for them. While capabilities presuppose the existence of resources and knowledge about how to transform them in a value-enhancing manner within a functional area of the firm, competencies presuppose the existence of capabilities and the knowledge about how to interconnect them in a value-enhancing manner across functional areas of the firm. It is only by perfecting the underlying process of transformation of resources within functional areas, and the interconnection of capabilities across functional areas, through knowledge that firms can generate unique or superior core capabilities and competencies as a source of competitive advantage.

[39] While the view of firms as bundles of core capabilities is associated with the concept of ordinary capabilities and is rooted in the resource-based view of the firm, the view of firms as bundles of core capabilities aimed at exploring investments to hedge the future is associated with dynamic capabilities and is rooted in the knowledge-based view (Grant, 1996).

This begs the important question of whether knowledge is the fundamental unit of analysis, as knowledge-based theories of the firm may suggest (Grant, 1996; Kogut, 1996).

From an information theory standpoint, knowledge is defined as information plus a valuable use assigned to it (Devlin, 1999). As knowledge presupposes the existence of information, information is a precursor of knowledge and is therefore more fundamental. Information gives rise to knowledge only if the firm is able to find and assign valuable uses to that information for a clearly distinguishable group of potential clients and/or users (Devlin, 1999). Therefore, while knowledge is the precursor of resources, capabilities, and competencies, information is the precursor of knowledge and is the primordial asset of firms according to the informational view of the firm. The information realm in which dynamic metacapabilities operate deals with this fundamental problem of finding valuables uses for information.

The informational view of the firm we have introduced is aligned with the view of "firms as realizations of entrepreneurial visions" postulated by Witt (2007). The key question is where such "realization" begins. Witt construes this realization as "organizing resources into envisioned businesses" and presupposes the existence of an entrepreneur such that "resource owners must be coordinated on the entrepreneur's conception of the business" (Witt, 2007, p. 1125). While we concur with this author in that the existence of the entrepreneur, be it the entrepreneur of a start-up or the Teecean entrepreneurial manager of an incumbent firm, or the quantum manager of a start-up or an incumbent firm, is of the essence for firms to come into existence, the informational view of the firm presented in this contribution does not presuppose the existence of knowledge, resources, capabilities, or competencies.

The informational view of the firm postulates that firms exist, albeit only as "potentialities," as bundles of information. The challenge for a "potential" firm to come into existence lies in finding valuable uses for bundles of information as the primordial asset of the firm. Finding such valuable uses for bundles of information is an ongoing process that requires the deployment of dynamic metacapabilities and will eventually lead a "primordial firm," if successful, to the generation of core resources and capabilities not only as valuable, rare, inimitable, and non-substitutable resources and capabilities that are a source of competitive advantage but also as "capabilities embodying exploratory investments to hedge the future" (Kogut & Kulatikala, 2001, p. 747).

The question of how firms come into existence under the informational view of the firm is relevant not only for start-ups and emerging firms but also for incumbents. Our focus thus far on dynamic metacapabilities and incumbent firms is not due to the inability of start-up firms to deploy dynamic metacapabilities. It is rather due to the difficulties of incumbents to adopt the kind of entrepreneurial management that is characteristic of start-up firms. This type of entrepreneurial management is badly needed by incumbent firms to radically transform their business models and evolve in environments ridden with strategic uncertainty and organizational misalignment. But it is also difficult to implement by them (Christensen, 1997; Foster, 1986a).

Many of the real options used to operationalize dynamic metacapabilities, especially the alignment options, aim at allowing incumbent firms to adopt the kind of entrepreneurial management that is characteristic of start-ups and emerging firms (Teece, 2016). There is indeed abundant empirical evidence showing how emerging firms enjoy the so-called attacker's advantage vis-à-vis incumbent firms (Foster, 1986a). This advantage is associated with the dilemma of creative destruction that incumbents face when the need to destroy their still successful business models under deep strategic uncertainty arises. Start-ups and emerging firms are more agile, enjoy more flexibility to explore different innovation pathways and business models, and are therefore more prone to adopting the dynamic metacapabilities needed to transform a skeleton business model into a viable business model.

6.6 The Debate on Dynamic Capabilities

Underlying the dynamic metacapabilities framework there is the so-called dynamic metacapabilities lifecycle. This lifecycle allows us to reconcile the two competing views of dynamic capabilities (Eisenhardt & Martin, 2000; Teece, 2007). Although their boundaries are fuzzy, the distinction between ordinary and dynamic capabilities, on the one hand, and dynamic capabilities and dynamic metacapabilities, on the other, is facilitated following such a lifecycle approach.

Despite some significant differences, these two competing dynamic capabilities frameworks are both rooted in the resource-based view of the firm. They both construe dynamic capabilities as distinct from ordinary capabilities, which the resource-based view of the firm defines as those that are needed to achieve technical fitness in external environments that change at low or moderate velocity (Barney, 1991; Penrose, 1995; Wernerfelt, 1984). But there are important differences between them. Although there is an implicit lifecycle in the Teecean dynamic capabilities framework, which would comprise three phases, namely, sensing, seizing, and transforming, both frameworks do not explicitly propose a lifecycle of dynamic capabilities (Eisenhardt & Martin, 2000; Teece, 2007).

While the Teecean framework leaves dynamic capabilities underspecified, which according to Eisenhardt & Martin (2000) renders the Teecean dynamic capabilities rather tautological and vague, Eisenhardt and Martin (2000) describe what dynamic capabilities are by extension and propose that "rather than tautological, vague, and lacking empirical grounding, dynamic capabilities are concrete capabilities that have been studied in several management areas, such as product innovation management and strategic alliances" (Eisenhardt & Martin, 2000, p. 1106).

Instead of proposing an actual framework, Eisenhardt and Martin (2000) describe dynamic capabilities as fungible, substitutable, and ultimately equifinal. They also characterize them as best industry practices that are rapidly adopted by competitors. Dynamic capabilities, as described by Eisenhardt and Martin (2000), are thus unable to provide a source of sustainable competitive advantage and can only deliver a temporary competitive advantage in high-velocity markets, which is a view shared by other strategic management scholars (D'Aveni, 1994; D'Aveni, Dagnino, & Smith, 2010).

Rather than two competing dynamic capabilities frameworks, we argue that these are two complementary frameworks of capabilities. Key to understanding the difference between them is the realization that ordinary and dynamic capabilities, and dynamic metacapabilities, operate in phases of the lifecycle of dynamic metacapabilities dominated by different levels of strategic uncertainty and organizational misalignment.

6.7 Future Work

Future work will focus on extending the dynamic metacapabilities framework by adding new real options under the three classes of real options proposed, on developing valuation models for the real options in these three classes, and on formalizing the boundary conditions for decoherence and collapse based on multicriteria decision analysis methods and tools to guide complex quantum management decisions along the lifecycle of dynamic metacapabilities.

The development of decision-theoretic models and methods in the aforementioned areas represents a major challenge and will be based not on utility theory (von Neumann & Morgenstern, 1944) and subjective utility theory (Fishburn, 1981, 1986) but rather on more modern theories in behavioral economics that draw upon the psychology of human decision-making under risk, such as prospect theory (Kahneman & Tversky, 1979; Tversky & Kahneman,

1992) and regret theory (Loomes & Sugden, 1982). Future work in these areas is highly relevant because, as noted by Teece (2007, p. 1329), "strategic management decisions are often impaired by the lack of visibility into the criteria under which to evaluate cospecialized and complementary intangible assets."

The dynamic metacapabilities framework, and its operationalization through quantum management, can also have a high impact on the future transformations toward sustainable economic systems in industries with conventional business models that have taken incumbents decades to develop, such as the automobile industry. The automobile industry is indeed a paradigmatic example of an industry where managers can apply quantum management to meet the challenge of throwing an old business model overboard[40] to develop innovative and sustainable (mobility) solutions. Future work will consist in applying quantum management to solve the complex trade-offs faced by managers driving business model transformations toward sustainability in this and other industries.

We will also embark on a research agenda at the intersection of dynamic metacapabilities and digital platforms. Digital platforms have given rise to a new economic model referred to as "the global stakeholder capitalism model of digital platforms" (Paredes-Frigolett & Pyka, 2022). The business models of digital platforms are currently disrupting the conventional "pipeline business models" of incumbents that still dominate large industries today (van Alstyne, Parker, & Choudary, 2016).[41] As their data-driven business models are poised to become the business models of the Industry 4.0 and beyond (Paredes-Frigolett & Pyka, 2023), digital platforms are already a testbed for the instantiation and deployment of dynamic metacapabilities. The research agenda we are proposing in this area is of the utmost relevance for understanding the role of dynamic metacapabilities in driving the strategy and implementing the business models of digital platforms as the business models of the Industry 4.0.

As gatekeepers of big data, the new fuel that is currently propelling the Industry 4.0 and is poised to propel the data-driven industrial revolutions that will follow, and with platform business models driven by the need to convert increasingly larger volumes of big data into information by assigning a meaning to data, and information into knowledge by finding valuable uses for

40 A business model based on the Fordist mass production system in the case of the car industry.

41 The grand strategy of Google under Alphabet is a quintessential example of such disruption and is not an isolated case, as the new grand strategy of Facebook under Meta Platforms shows.

new information, digital platforms are already living examples of the informational view of the firm. They are also in a privileged position not only to deploy dynamic metacapabilities and benefit from quantum management to enter industries still dominated today by incumbents with conventional "pipeline business models" rooted in the resourced-based view of the firm but also to disrupt these industries with platform business models rooted in the informational view of the firm, as introduced in this contribution to the Elements Series in Evolutionary Economics.

References

Abdelkafi, N., & Täuscher, K. (2016). Business models for sustainability from a systems dynamics perspective. *Organization & Environment, 29*(1), 74–96.

Ahrweiler, P. (2010). *Innovation in Complex Social Systems*. New York: Routledge.

Amit, R., & Shoemaker, P. (1993). Strategic assets and organizational rent. *Strategic Management Journal, 14*(1), 33–46.

Amit, R., & Zott, C. (2001). Value creation in e-business. *Strategic Management Journal, 22*(6–7), 493–520.

Anthony, S. (2016). Kodak's downfall wasn't about technology. *Harvard Business Review*. https://hbr.org/2016/07/kodaks-downfall-wasnt-about-technology.

Aoki, K., & Lennerfors, T. (2013). The new, improved keiretsu. *Harvard Business Review, 91*(9), 109–113.

Arthur, C. (2012). *Digital Wars: Apple, Google, Microsoft and the Battle for the Internet*. London: Kogan Page.

Aspara, J., Lamberg, J., Laukia, A., & Tikkanen, H. (2013). Corporate business model transformation and interorganizational cognition. *Long Range Planning, 46*(6), 459–474.

Baden-Fuller, C., & Haefliger, S. (2013). Business models and technological innovation. *Long Range Planning, 46*(6), 419–426.

Baden-Fuller, C., & Morgan, M. (2010). Business models as models. *Long Range Planning, 43*(2–3), 156–171.

Barney, J. (1991). Firms resources and sustained competitive advantage. *Journal of Management, 17*(1), 99–120.

Birkinshaw, J., & Goddard, J. (2009). What is your management model? *Sloan Management Review, 50*(2), 81–90.

Bocken, N., Rana, P., & Short, S. (2015). Value mapping for sustainable business thinking? *Journal of Industrial and Production Engineering, 32*(1), 67–81.

Bogers, M., Chesbrough, H., & Moedas, C. (2018). Open innovation: Research, practices, and policies. *California Management Review, 60*(2), 5–16.

Boons, F., & Lüdecke-Freund, F. (2013). Business models for sustainable innovation: State-of-the-art and steps towards a research agenda. *Journal of Cleaner Production, 45*, 9–19.

Bowman, E., & Moskowitz, G. (2001). Real options analysis and strategic decision making. *Organization Science, 12*(6), 772–777.

Cain, G. (2020). Samsung vs. Apple: Inside the brutal war for smartphone dominance. *Forbes*. https://www.forbes.com/sites/forbesdigitalcovers/2020/03/13/samsung-vs-apple-inside-the-brutal-war-for-smartphone-dominance/#3f00eec64142.

Callaham, J. (2018). Google made its best acquisition 13 years ago: Can you guess what it was? *Android Authority*. https://www.androidauthority.com/google-android-acquisition-884194/.

Camerer, C. (2003). Behavioural studies of strategic thinking in games. *Trends in Cognitive Science*, *7*(5), 225–231.

Camerer, C. (2005). Three cheers – psychological, theoretical, empirical–for loss aversion. *Journal of Marketing Research*, *42*(2), 129–133.

Carlson, C., & Wilmot, W. (2006). *The Five Disciplines for Creating What Customers Want*. New York: Crown.

Casadesus-Masanell, R., & Ricart, J. (2010). From strategy to business models and onto tactics. *Long-Range Planning*, *43*(2–3), 195–215.

Casadesus-Masanell, R., & Zhu, F. (2013). Business model innovation and competitive imitation: The case of sponsor-based business models. *Strategic Management Journal*, *34*(4), 464–482.

Chesbrough, H. (2003). *Open Innovation: The New Imperative for Creating and Profiting from Technology*. Boston, MA: Harvard Business School Press.

Chesbrough, H. (2007). Business model innovation: It's not just about technology anymore. *Strategy and Leadership*, *35*(6), 12–17.

Chesbrough, H. (2010). Business model innovation: Opportunities and barriers. *Long Range Planning*, *43*(2–3), 354–363.

Chesbrough, H., & Rosensbloom, R. (2002). The role of the business model in capturing value from innovation: Evidence from Xerox Corporation's technology spinoff companies. *Industrial and Corporate Change*, *11*(3), 529–555.

Christensen, C. (1997). *The Innovator's Dilemma: When New Technologies Cause Great Firms to Fail*. Boston, MA: Harvard University Press.

Cooper, R. (2008). The stage-gate idea-to-launch process update: What's new and next-generation systems. *Journal of Product Innovation Management*, *25*(3), 213–232.

Dahan, N., Doh, J., Oetzel, J., & Yaziji, M. (2010). Corporate-NGO collaboration: Co-creating new business models for developing markets. *Long-Range Planning*, *43*(2–3), 326–342.

D'Aveni, R. (1994). *Hypercompetition: Managing the Dynamics of Strategic Maneuvering*. New York: The Free Press.

D'Aveni, R., Dagnino, G., & Smith, K. (2010). The age of temporary advantage. *Strategic Management Journal*, *31*(13), 1371–1385.

Demil, B., & Lecocq, X. (2010). Business model evolution: In search of dynamic consistency. *Long Range Planning, 43*(2–3), 227–246.

Devlin, K. (1999). *Infosense: Turning Information into Knowledge*. New York: W.H. Freeman.

Doganova, L., & Eyquem-Renault, M. (2009). What do business model do? Innovation devices in technology entrepreneurship. *Research Policy, 38*(10), 1559–1570.

Doz, Y., & Kosonen, M. (2010). Embedding strategic agility: A leadership agenda for accelerating business model renewal. *Long Range Planning, 43*(2–3), 370–382.

Eisenhardt, K., & Martin, J. (2000). Dynamic capabilities: What are they? *Strategic Management Journal, 21*(10–11), 1105–1121.

Ferrary, M., & Granovetter, M. (2009). The role of venture capital firms in Silicon Valley's complex innovation network. *Economy and Society, 38*(2), 326–359.

Fishburn, P. (1981). Subjective expected utility: A review of normative theories. *Theory and Decision, 13*, 139–199.

Fishburn, P. (1986). The axioms of subjective probability. *Statistical Science, 1*(3), 335–345.

Foster, R. (1986a). *Innovation: The Attacker's Advantage*. New York: Summit Books.

Foster, R. (1986b). *The S Curve: A New Forecasting Tool*. London: Macmillan.

Frydman, C., & Camerer, C. (2016). The psychology and neuroscience of financial decision making. *Trends in Cognitive Science, 20*(9), 661–675.

Gambardella, A., & McGahan, A. (2010). Business model innovation: General purpose technologies and their implications for industry structure. *Long-Range Planning, 43*(2–3), 262–271.

Gompers, P., & Lerner, J. (2004). *The Venture Capital Cycle*. Cambridge, MA: MIT Press.

Grant, R. (1996). Toward a knowledge-based theory of the firm. *Strategic Management Journal, 17*(S2), 109–122.

Hay, D., & Morris, D. (1991). *Industrial Economics and Organization: Theory and Evidence*. Oxford: Oxford University Press.

Helfat, C., Finkelstein, S., Mitchell, W., et al. (2007). *Dynamic Capabilities: Understanding Strategic Change in Organizations*. Oxford: Blackwell.

Helfat, C., & Peteraf, M. (2003). The dynamic resourced-based view: Capability lifecycles. *Strategic Management Journal, 24*(10), 997–1010.

Hienerth, C., Keinz, P., & Lettl, C. (2011). Exploring the nature and implementation process of user-centric business models. *Long-Range Planning, 44*(5–6), 344–374.

Itami, H., & Nishino, K. (2010). Killing one bird with one stone: Profit for now and learning for the future. *Long Range Planning*, *43*(2–3), 364–369.

Johnson, M., Christensen, C., & Kagermann, H. (2008). Reinventing your business model. *Harvard Business Review*, *86*(12), 52–60.

Kahneman, D., & Tversky, A. (1979). Prospect theory: An analysis of decision under risk. *Econometrica*, *47*(2), 263–292.

Kay, J., & King, M. (2020). *Radical Uncertainty: Decision-Making Beyond the Numbers*. New York: W.W. Norton.

Kogut, B. (1996). What firms do? Coordination, identity, and learning. *Organization Science*, *7*(5), 502–518.

Kogut, B., & Kulatikala, N. (2001). Capabilities as real options. *Organization Science*, *12*(6), 744–758.

Kogut, B., & Kulatilaka, N. (1994). Options thinking and platform investments: Investing in opportunity. *California Management Review*, *36*(2), 52–71.

Lamberg, J.- A., Lubinaité, S., Ojala, J., & Tikkanen, H. (2019). The curse of agility: The Nokia Corporation and the loss of market dominance in mobile phones, 2003–2013. *Business History*, *63*(4), 574–605.

Loasby, B. (1967). Management economics and the theory of the firm. *The Journal of Industrial Economics*, *15*(3), 165–176.

Loasby, B. (1990). Firms, markets, and the principle of continuity. In John K. Whitaker (Ed.), *Centenary Essays on Alfred Marshall* (pp. 108–126). Cambridge: Cambridge University Press.

Loomes, G., & Sugden, R. (1982). Regret theory: An alternative theory of rational choice under uncertainty. *The Economic Journal*, *92*(368), 805–824.

Luehrman, T. (1988). Strategy as a portfolio of real options. *Harvard Business Review*, *76*(5), 89–99.

Macher, J., & Mowery, D. (2005). Vertical specialization and industry structure in high technology industries. *Advances in Strategic Management*, *21*, 317–355.

Magretta, J. (2002). Why business models matter. *Harvard Business Review*, *80*(5), 86–92.

Mahoney, J., & Pandian, J. (1992). The resource-based view within the conversation of strategic management. *Strategic Management Journal*, *13*(5), 363–380.

Manjoo, F. (2015). With Google as Alphabet, a bid to dream big beyond search. *The New York Times*. https://www.nytimes.com/2015/08/11/technology/giving-google-room-to-dream-big-beyond-search.html?_r=0.

Markides, C., & Oyon, D. (2010). What to do against disruptive business models (when and how to play two games at once). *MIT Sloan Management Review*, 52(4), 25–32.

Markides, C., & Sosa, L. (2013). Pioneering and first mover advantages: The importance of business models. *Long Range Planning*, *46*(4–5), 325–334.

Martins, L., Rindova, V., & Greenbaum, B. (2015). Unlocking the hidden value of concepts: A cognitive approach to business model innovation. *Strategic Entrepreneurship Journal*, *9*(1), 99–117.

Massa, L., Tucci, C., & Afuah, A. (2017). A critical assessment of business model research. *Academy of Management Annals*, *11*(1), 73–104.

McCray, J. P., Gonzalez, J. J., & Darling, J. R. (2011). Crisis management in smart phones: The case of Nokia vs Apple. *European Business Review*, *23*(3), 240–255.

McGrath, R. (1997). A real options logic for initiating technology positioning investments. *Academy of Management Review*, *22*(4), 974–996.

McGrath, R. (1999). Falling forward: Real options reasoning and entrepreneurial failures. *Academy of Management Review*, *24*(1), 13–30.

McGrath, R. (2010). Business models: A discovery driven approach. *Long Range Planning*, *43*(2–3), 247–261.

Miller, M., & Modigliani, F. (1961). Dividend policy, growth, and the valuation of shares. *Journal of Business*, *34*(4), 411–433.

Nelson, R. (1991). Why do firms differ, and how does it matter? *Strategic Management Journal*, *12*(S2), 61–74.

Nelson, R. (2018). Economics from an evolutionary perspective. In Nelson, R. R., Dosi, G., Helfat C. E., et al. (Eds.), *Modern Evolutionary Economics: An Overview* (pp. 1–34). Cambridge: Cambridge University Press.

Nelson, R., & Winter, S. (1982). *An Evolutionary Theory of Economic Change*. Cambridge, MA: Belknap Press.

Nickerson, R., Varshney, U., & Muntermann, J. (2013). A method for taxonomy development and its application in information systems. *European Journal of Information Systems*, *22*(3), 336–359.

Nielsen, C., & Lund, M. (2014). An introduction to business models. In Nielsen, C., & Lund, M. (Eds.), *The Basics of Business Models* (pp. 8–20). Copenhagen: Bookboon. https://bookboon.com/en/the-basics-of-business-models-ebook.

Normann, R. (2001). *Reframing Business: When the Map Changes the Landscape*. Chichester: John Wiley & Sons.

Osterwalder, A., & Pigneur, Y. (2010). *Business Model Generation: A Handbook for Visionaries, Game Changers, and Challengers*. Hoboken: Wiley.

Osterwalder, A., Pigneur, Y., & Tucci, C. (2005). Clarifying business models: Origins, present, and future of the concept. *Communications of the Association for Information Systems*, *16*, 1–25.

Paredes-Frigolett, H., & Pyka, A. (2015). A generic innovation network formation strategy. In Foster, J. & Pyka, A. (Eds.), *Co-Evolution and Complex Adaptive Systems in Evolutionary Economics, Springer Series Economic Complexity and Evolution* (pp. 279–308). Zurich: Springer.

Paredes-Frigolett, H., & Pyka, A. (2022). The global stakeholder capitalism model of digital platforms and its implications for strategy and innovation from a Schumpeterian perspective. *Journal of Evolutionary Economics, 32*(2), 463–500.

Paredes-Frigolett, H., & Pyka, A. (2023). Global dematerialization, the renaissance of Artificial Intelligence, and the global stakeholder capitalism model of digital platforms: Current challenges and future directions. *Journal of Evolutionary Economics, 33*(3), 671–705.

Parker, G., van Alstyne, M., & Choudary, S. (2016). *Platform Revolution: How Networked Markets Are Transforming the Economy – and How to Make Them Work for You.* New York: Norton.

Peng, M., & Wang, D. (2000). Innovation capability and foreign direct investment: Toward a learning option perspective. *Management International Review, 40*(1), 79–93.

Penrose, E. (1959). *The Theory of the Growth of the Firm.* New York: Wiley.

Penrose, E. (1995). *The Theory of the Growth of the Firm (Third Edition).* Oxford: Oxford University Press.

Peteraf, M. (1993). The cornerstones of competitive advantage. *Strategic Management Journal, 14*(3), 179–191.

Pisano, G., Shan, W., & Teece, D. (1988). Joint ventures and collaboration in the biotechnology industry. In Mowery, D. (Ed.), *International Collaborative Ventures in U.S. Manufacturing* (pp. 183–222). Cambridge, MA: Ballinger.

Porter, M. (2008). The five competitive forces that shape strategy. Special issue on HBS Centennial. *Harvard Business Review, 86*(1), 78–93.

Provance, M., Donnely, R., & Carayannis, E. (2011). Institutional influences on business model choice by new ventures in the micro-generated energy industry. *Energy Policy, 39*(9), 5630–5637.

Pyka, A. (2002). Innovation networks in economics: From the incentive-based to the knowledge-based approaches. *European Journal of Innovation Management, 5*(3), 152–163.

Pyka, A., & Saviotti, P.- P. (2005). The evolution of R&D networking in the biotech industries. *International Journal of Entrepreneurship and Innovation Management, 5*(1/2), 49–68.

Reim, W., Parida, V., & Örtqvist, D. (2015). Product-Service Systems (PSS) business models and tactics: A systematic literature review. *Journal of Cleaner Production, 97*, 61–75.

Ritter, T. (2014). *Alignment^2 [Alignment Squared]: Driving Competitiveness and Growth through Business Model Excellence*. Copenhagen: The CBS Competitiveness Platform.

Romero, E., Novoderezhkin, V., & van Grondelle, R. (2017). Quantum design of photosynthesis for bio-inspired solar-energy conversion. *Nature, 543*(7645), 355–365.

Roome, N., & Louche, C. (2016). Journeying toward business model for sustainability: A conceptual model found inside the black box of organisational transformation. *Organization and Environment*, *29*(1), 11–35.

Roth, E., & Peter, J. (2023). Google's big AI push will combine Brain and DeepMind into one team. *The Verge*. https://www.theverge.com/2023/4/20/23691468/google-ai-deepmind-brain-merger.

Roy, B., & Bertier, P. (1996). *Multicriteria Methodology for Decision Aiding*. Netherlands: Kluwer Academic.

Sakurai, J., & Napolitano, J. (2020). *Modern Quantum Mechanics (Third Edition)* Cambridge: Cambridge University Press.

San Román, T., Momber, I., Abbad, M., & Miralles, A. (2011). Regulatory frameworks and business models for charging plug-in electric vehicles: Infrastructure, agents, and commercial relationships. *Energy Policy*, *39*(10), 6360–6375.

Savov, C. V. (2017). Windows phone was a glorious failure. *The Verge*. https://www.theverge.com/2017/10/10/16452162/windows-phone-history-glorious-failure.

Schaltegger, S., Hansen, E., & Lüdecke-Freund, F. (2016). Business models for sustainability: Origins, present research, and future avenues. *Organization & Environment*, *29*(1), 3–10.

Schumpeter, J. A. (1942). *Capitalism, Socialism and Democracy*. London: George Allen & Unwin.

Shannon, C. (1948). A mathematical theory of communication. *Bell Systems Technology Journal*, *27*(3), 379–423.

Sheehan, M. (2018). How Google took on China – and lost. *MIT Technology Review*. https://www.technologyreview.com/2018/12/19/138307/how-google-took-on-china-and-lost/.

Shih, S. (2016). The real lessons from Kodak's decline. *MIT Sloan Management Review*, *57*(4), 11–13.

Simon, H. (1962). The architecture of complexity. *Proceedings of the American Philosophical Society*, *106*(6), 467–482.

Sinfield, J., Calder, E., McConnell, B., & Colson, S. (2012). How to identify new business models. *MIT Sloan Management Review*, *53*(2), 85–90.

Smith, W., Binns, A., & Tushman, M. (2010). Complex business models: Managing strategic paradoxes simultaneously. *Long Range Planning*, *43*(2–3), 448–461.

Sorenson, O., & Stuart, T. (2001). Syndication networks and the spatial distribution of venture capital investments. *American Journal of Sociology*, *106*(6), 1546–1588.

Sorenson, O., & Stuart, T. (2008). Bridging the context back in: Settings and the search for syndicate partners in venture capital investments networks. *Administrative Science Quarterly*, *53*(2), 266–294.

Teece, D. (1976). *Vertical Integration and Vertical Divestiture in the U.S. Oil Industry*. Working Paper No 300. Stanford, CA: Stanford Graduate School of Business. https://www.gsb.stanford.edu/faculty-research/working-papers/vertical-integration-vertical-divestiture-us-petroleum-industry.

Teece, D. (1986). Profiting from technological innovation: Implications for integration, collaboration, licensing and public policy. *Research Policy*, *15*(6), 285–305.

Teece, D. (2006). Reflections on "Profiting from Innovation." *Research Policy*, *35*(8), 1131–1146.

Teece, D. (2007). Explicating dynamic capabilities: The nature and microfoundations of (sustainable) enterprise performance. *Strategic Management Journal*, *28*(13), 1319–1350.

Teece, D. (2010). Business models, business strategy and innovation. *Long Range Planning*, *43*(2–3), 172–194.

Teece, D. (2016). Dynamic capabilities and entrepreneurial management in large organizations: Toward a theory of the (entrepreneurial) firm. *European Economic Review*, *86*, 202–216.

Teece, D. (2018a). Profiting from innovation in the digital economy: Enabling technologies, standards, and licensing models in the wireless world. *Research Policy*, *47*(8), 1367–1387.

Teece, D. (2018b). Reply to Nelson, Helfat and Raubitschek. *Research Policy*, *47*(8), 1400–1402.

Teece, D. (2018c). Tesla and the reshaping of the auto industry. *Management and Organization Review*, *14*(3), 501–512.

Teece, D. (2023). Evolutionary economics, routines, and dynamic capabilities. In Dopfer, K., Nelson, R. R., Potts, J., & Pyka, A. (Eds.), *Routledge Handbook of Evolutionary Economics* (pp. 197–214). London: Routledge.

Teece, D., & Pisano, G. (1994). The dynamic capabilities of enterprises: An introduction. *Industrial and Corporate Change*, *3*(3), 537–556.

Teece, D., Pisano, G., & Shuen, A. (1990). *Enterprise capabilities, resources and the concept of strategy*. University of California at Berkeley (CA):

Consortium on Competitiveness and Cooperation, Working Paper CCC-90–98, Institute of Management, Innovation and Organization.

Teece, D., Pisano, G., & Shuen, A. (1997). Dynamic capabilities and strategic management. *Strategic Management Journal, 18*(7), 509–533.

Trigeorgis, L., & Reuer, J. (2017). Real options theory in strategic management. *Strategic Management Journal, 38*(1), 42–63.

Tversky, A., & Kahneman, D. (1992). Advances in prospect theory, cumulative representation of uncertainty. *Journal of Risk and Uncertainty, 5*(4), 297–323.

Upward, A., & Jones, P. (2015). An ontology for strongly sustainable business models defining an enterprise framework compatible with natural and social science. *Organization & Environment, 29*(1), 97–123.

van Alstyne, M., Parker, G., & Choudary, S. (2016). Pipelines, platforms, and the new rules of strategy. *Harvard Business Review, 94*(4), 54–62.

Vasallo, A., & Romano, D. (2023). The metaphysics of decoherence. *Erkenntnis, 88*(6), 2609–2631.

Velu, C., & Stiles, P. (2013). Managing decision-making and cannibalization for parallel business models. *Long Range Planning, 46*(6), 443–458.

von Neumann, J. (2018). *Mathematical Foundations of Quantum Mechanics (New Edition)*. New Jersey, NJ: Princeton University Press.

von Neumann, J., & Morgenstern, O. (1944). *Theory of Games and Economic Behavior*. Princeton, NJ: Princeton University Press.

Vuori, T. O., & Huy, Q. N. (2016). Distributed attention and shared emotions in the innovation process: How Nokia lost the smartphone battle. *Administrative Science Quarterly, 61*(1), 9–51.

Weill, P., Malone, T., & Apel, T. (2011). The business models investors prefer. *MIT Sloan Management Review, 52*(4), 17–19.

Welch, C. (2019). Google begins shutting down its failed Google+ social network. *The Verge*. https://www.theverge.com/2019/4/2/18290637/google-plus-shutdown-consumer-personal-account-delete.

Wells, P. (2016). Economies of scale versus small is beautiful: A business model approach based on architecture, principles and components in the beer industry. *Organization & Environment, 29*(1), 36–52.

Wernerfelt, B. (1984). A resource-based view of the firm. *Strategic Management Journal, 5*(2), 171–180.

Wernerfelt, B. (1995). The resource-based view of the firm: Ten years after. *Strategic Management Journal, 68*(3), 171–174.

Winter, S. (2003). Understanding dynamic capabilities. *Strategic Management Journal, 24*(10), 991–995.

Winter, S. (2006). Toward a neo-Schumpeterian theory of the firm. *Industrial and Corporate Change, 15*(1), 125–141.

Wirtz, B., Schilke, O., & Ullrich, S. (2010). Strategic development of business models: Implications of the Web 2.0 for creating value on the Internet. *Long Range Planning*, *43*(2–3), 272–290.

Witt, U. (2007). Firms as realizations of entrepreneurial visions. *Journal of Management Studies*, *44*(7), 1125–1140.

Yunus, M., Moingeon, B., & Lehmann-Ortega, L. (2010). Building social business models: Lessons from the Grameen experience. *Long Range Planning*, *43*(2–3), 308–325.

Zeh, H. (1970). On the interpretation of measurement in quantum theory. *Foundations in Physics*, *1*(1), 69–76.

Zopounidis, C., & Pardalos, P. (2010). *Handbook of Multicriteria Analysis*. Heidelberg: Springer Verlag.

Zott, C., & Amit, R. (2010). Business model design: An activity system perspective. *Long Range Planning*, *43*(2–3), 216–226.

Zott, C., Amit, R., & Massa, L. (2011). The business model: Recent developments and future research. *Journal of Management*, *37*(4), 1019–1042.

Zureck, W. H. (2018). Quantum reversibility is relative, or does a quantum measurement reset initial conditions? *Philosophical Transactions of the Royal Society A*, *376*(2123), 20170315.

Cambridge Elements

Evolutionary Economics

About the Series

Cambridge Elements of Evolutionary Economics provides authoritative and up-to-date reviews of core topics and recent developments in the field. It includes state-of-the-art contributions on all areas in the field. The series is broadly concerned with questions of dynamics and change, with a particular focus on processes of entrepreneurship and innovation, industrial and institutional dynamics, and on patterns of economic growth and development.

Cambridge Elements

Evolutionary Economics

Elements in the Series

A full series listing is available at: www.cambridge.org/EEVE

For EU product safety concerns, contact us at Calle de José Abascal, 56–1°, 28003 Madrid, Spain or eugpsr@cambridge.org.

www.ingramcontent.com/pod-product-compliance
Ingram Content Group UK Ltd.
Pitfield, Milton Keynes, MK11 3LW, UK
UKHW022145080726
473066UK00010B/774

* 9 7 8 1 0 0 9 6 2 7 6 3 4 *